LEARNING ENGLISH

A TV/VIDEO INDEPENDENT STUDY PROGRAM IN ENGLISH AS A SECOND LANGUAGE

Lori Howard • Norma Shapiro • Elaine Sunoo
Illustrated by Marty Murphy

LOS ANGELES UNIFIED SCHOOL DISTRICT
Division of Adult and Occupational Education
Adult ESL/Amnesty and Citizenship Programs

 DELTA SYSTEMS CO., INC.

Copyright © 1992 by Delta Systems Co., Inc.

ISBN 0-937354-76-7

All rights reserved. No part of this
publication may be reproduced, stored in a
retrieval system, or transmitted, in any form
or by any means, mechanical, electronic,
recording, photocopying, or otherwise,
without the prior permission of
Delta Systems Co., Inc.

This book is sold subject to the condition that
it shall not, by way of trade or otherwise, be
lent, re-sold, hired out, or otherwise
circulated without the publisher's prior
consent in any form of binding or cover other
than that in which it is published and
without a similar condition including this
condition being imposed on the
subsequent purchaser.

Printed in the United States.

Acknowledgments

The contributions of the following persons in the development of the *Learning English* textbook are gratefully acknowledged:

    Bill Austin, Print Art
    Ed Costales, Cover Art
    Michael McLaughlin, Copy Editing
    Amy Schneider, Copy Editing
    Andre Sutton, Graphic Design and Typesetting
    Jeff Vollmer, Graphic Design and Typesetting

This text is based on the *Learning English* TV/Video Series written and taught by Sharon Hilles, Lori Howard and Ricardo Rodriguez. Many thanks to them and to the following persons: Curriculum Advisory Committee members, Jayme Adelson-Goldstein, Ann Creighton, Paul Hamel, Bob Harper, Greta Kojima and Carol Mares; Sadae Iwataki, Supervisor, Adult ESL Programs (retired); Dr. Patricia Prescott Marshall, Assistant Superintendent, Media Services; and Gabriel Cortina, Assistant Superintendent, Region E.

    Domingo A. Rodriguez
    Coordinator
    Adult ESL/Amnesty and
    Citizenship Programs

    Robert C. Rumin
    Director of Instruction
    Instructional Services Unit

Approved:

James A. Figueroa
Assistant Superintendent
Division of Adult and
Occupational Education

Contents

To the Student ...vi
To the Teacher ...viii

 **Unit 1** Making Friends ...1

 **Unit 6** Recreation and Leisure ...61

 **Unit 2** The Neighborhood ...13

 **Unit 7** Buying Clothing ...73

 **Unit 3** Health Care ...25

 **Unit 8** Getting a Job ...85

 **Unit 4** Looking for Housing ...37

 **Unit 9** On the Job ...97

 **Unit 5** Marketing ...49

 **Unit 10** Health and Fitness ...109

Contents

 **Unit 11**
Buying a Car ...121

 **Unit 16**
The Telephone ...181

 **Unit 12**
Apartment Living ...133

 **Unit 17**
Emergencies ...193

 **Unit 13**
Special Occasions ...145

 **Unit 18**
Schools ...205

 **Unit 14**
Getting Around the City ...157

 **Unit 19**
Driving a Car ...217

 **Unit 15**
Money ...169

 **Unit 20**
About Government ...229

v

To the Student

Welcome to *Learning English*!

- *Learning English* is a program to teach English as a Second Language to adults and young adults.

- *Learning English* will teach you real life listening, speaking, reading and writing skills.

- *Learning English* has 2 parts:
    1. 80 lessons you watch on TV or videotape. Each lesson is 30 minutes long.
    2. This textbook, which has 2 work pages to use with each lesson.

- To use *Learning English*:
    1. Watch the lesson on TV or videotape.
    2. Do the 2 work pages for that lesson in the textbook.
    3. Check your answers at the bottom of each page.
    4. After every 4 lessons, do the Review pages.

¡Bienvenidos a *Learning English*!

- *Learning English* es un programa que enseña inglés como segundo idioma a los adultos y a los jóvenes.

- *Learning English* le enseña acerca del uso del inglés en la vida real al escuchar, hablar, leer y escribir.

- *Learning English* tiene 2 partes:
    1. 80 lecciones que Ud. puede ver por televisión o en video "cassette". Cada lección dura 30 minutos.
    2. Este libro tiene 2 páginas de trabajo para cada lección.

- Para usar *Learning English*:
    1. Vea la lección en la televisión o en video "cassette".
    2. Haga las 2 páginas de trabajo para esa lección en el libro.
    3. Revise sus respuestas al fondo de la página.
    4. Después de cada 4 lecciones, haga las páginas de "Review".

歡迎來學習英語：

- 學習英語是教青年人與成人英語為第二種語言的一項節目。

- 學習英語可以教您在日常生活中聽講閱讀與寫的能力。

- 學習英語分為二部份：
    1. 電視與錄影帶教學，有八十課程。每一課程有卅分鐘長。
    2. 每一課程，教科書有二頁作習題。

- 如何應用學習英語：
    1. 利用電視或錄影帶上課。
    2. 每一課程後作教科書內二頁的作習題。
    3. 校對你的答案有正確答案在每頁底與你的答案校對。
    4. 每四個課程作複習題。

영어학습에 참여하는 것을 환영합니다.

- 영어학습은 성인과 젊은 학생들에게 영어를 제2외국어로 가르치는 프로그램입니다.
- 영어학습은 여러분에게 실제생활에서 듣고, 말하고, 읽고 그리고 쓰는 기능을 가르칩니다.
- 영어학습에는 두 부분으로 되어 있습니다.
  1. 텔리비젼이나 비디오로 보고 배우는 80학과목이 있고, 각학과는 30분짜리입니다.
  2. 각학과나 같이 쓰일 2페이지로 된 교재가 있습니다.
- 영어학습이용
  1. 텔리비젼이나 비디오로 학과를 보고 배움.
  2. 두 페이지로 된 교재의 학과를 공부할 것.
  3. 답을 점검할 것.
  4. 매 4학과를 마친후 복습 페이지를 공부할 것.

Բարի եկաք ԱՆԳԼԵՐԵՆ ՍՈՐՎԻԼ դասընթացքներուն:

- ԱՆԳԼԵՐԵՆ ՍՈՐՎԻԼ ծրագիր մըն է՝ չափահասներուն եւ պատանիներուն Անգլերէն սորվեցնելու:
- ԱՆԳԼԵՐԵՆ ՍՈՐՎԻԼ-ը ձեզի պիտի սորվեցնէ ունկնդրելու, խօսելու, գրելու եւ կարդալու առօրեայ հմտութիւնը:
- ԱՆԳԼԵՐԵՆ ՍՈՐՎԻԼ-ը կը բաղկանայ 2 մասերէ՝
  1. 80 դասեր, իւրաքանչիւրը 80 վայրկեան տեւողութեամբ, որ կրնաք ունկնդրել հեռուստացոյցով կամ տեսաներիզով:
  2. Այս դասագիրքը, որ իւրաքանչիւր դասի հետ ունի 2 աշխատանքի էջեր:
- ԱՆԳԼԵՐԵՆ ՍՈՐՎԻԼ-ը գործածելու համար՝
  1. Դասը դիտել հեռուստացոյցով կամ տեսաներիզով:
  2. Դասագրքին մէջ, այդ դասին պատկանող 2 աշխատանքի էջերը ամբողջացնել:
  3. Ձեր պատասխանները ստուգել:
  4. Ամէն 4 դասի վերջաւորութեան, լրացնել վերաքաղի էջերը:

For *Learning English* broadcast information or to obtain videotapes, call or write:

Para información sobre la transmisión de los programas de *Learning English* o para obtener video "cassettes", llame o escriba a:

如果你想了解學習英語的廣播資料或如何得到教學錄影帶請來信或來電。

영어학습을 위해 방송안내와 비디오테이프를 얻고저 하면 다음 부서로 전화를 하거나 서면으로 조회하시기 바람.

ԱՆԳԼԵՐԵՆ ՍՈՐՎԻԼ դասընթացքներու հեռուստացոյցի ժամերու եւ կամ տեսաներիզի մասին տեղեկութիւն ստանալու համար գրել կամ հեռաձայնել՝

DELTA SYSTEMS CO., INC.

To the Teacher

Learning English is a series of TV/video lessons and this accompanying textbook which use real-life situations to teach English as a Second Language. Adults and young adults at the beginning levels can use this independent study program to practice listening, speaking, reading and writing.

Each of the 80 half-hour TV/video lessons corresponds to two work pages in the textbook. Lessons are grouped into 20 units (4 lessons per unit), each focusing on a different life skill. The textbook provides a review section at the end of each unit.

Learning English makes it simple for students to study independently. The textbook uses easily understood symbols to guide the student through the lesson. In addition, the illustrations in the textbook mirror the visual aids used in the TV/video lesson to help students match what they are reading in the text with what they have learned during the TV/video lesson. To facilitate self-correction, the answers to the exercises appear at the bottom of each page.

Learning English is designed to allow students to learn independently. However, the addition of a teacher or tutor can make the program even more effective. Also, the program is well suited for use in a multilevel classroom with one group studying *Learning English* independently while the teacher directs another group.

Unit 1

Making Friends

Lesson 1a

Objectives
say "hello"
introduce yourself
say "good-bye"

Nice to meet you.
Glad to meet you.

Nice to meet you.
Nice to meet you, too.

Glad to meet you.
Glad to meet you, too.

Making Friends

Glad to meet you too

Mary:	Hi. My __name__ is Mary Jones.	
Tom:	Hi. My __name__ is Tom Johnson.	
Mary:	Nice to __meet__ you.	
Tom:	__Nice__ to meet you.	
Mary:	Tom Johnson, this is Sam Smith.	
Tom:	Nice __to__ meet you.	
Sam:	Glad to meet __you__.	
Mary:	It's __late__. I have to go. Good-bye.	
Tom:	See you __later__.	
Sam:	Good-bye.	

Answers: 1. name 2. name 3. meet 4. Glad 5. to 6. you 7. late 8. later

Making Friends

She's a __student__. He's a __teacher__. He's a __busboy__.
      1.   2.   3.

He's a __mechanic__. She's a __doctor__. She's a __nurse__.
      4.   5.   6.

He's a __gardener__. I'm a __Sofia__.
      7.   8.

Anna Lopez   Bob Ly   (you)
El Salvador   Vietnam

Where is she from?   **Where is he from?**   **Where are you from?**
She's from __El Salvador__.   He's from __Vietnam__.   I'm from __Cuba__.
      9.   10.   11.

Answers: 1. student 2. teacher 3. busboy 4. mechanic 5. doctor 6. nurse 7. gardener
8. (your occupation) 9. El Salvador 10. Vietnam 11. (your country)

Lesson 1c

Objectives say your telephone number
say your address
fill out a form

What's your telephone number?

It's (__ __ __) __ __ __ - __ __ __ __.
           1.

What's your area code?

It's __ __ __.
       2.

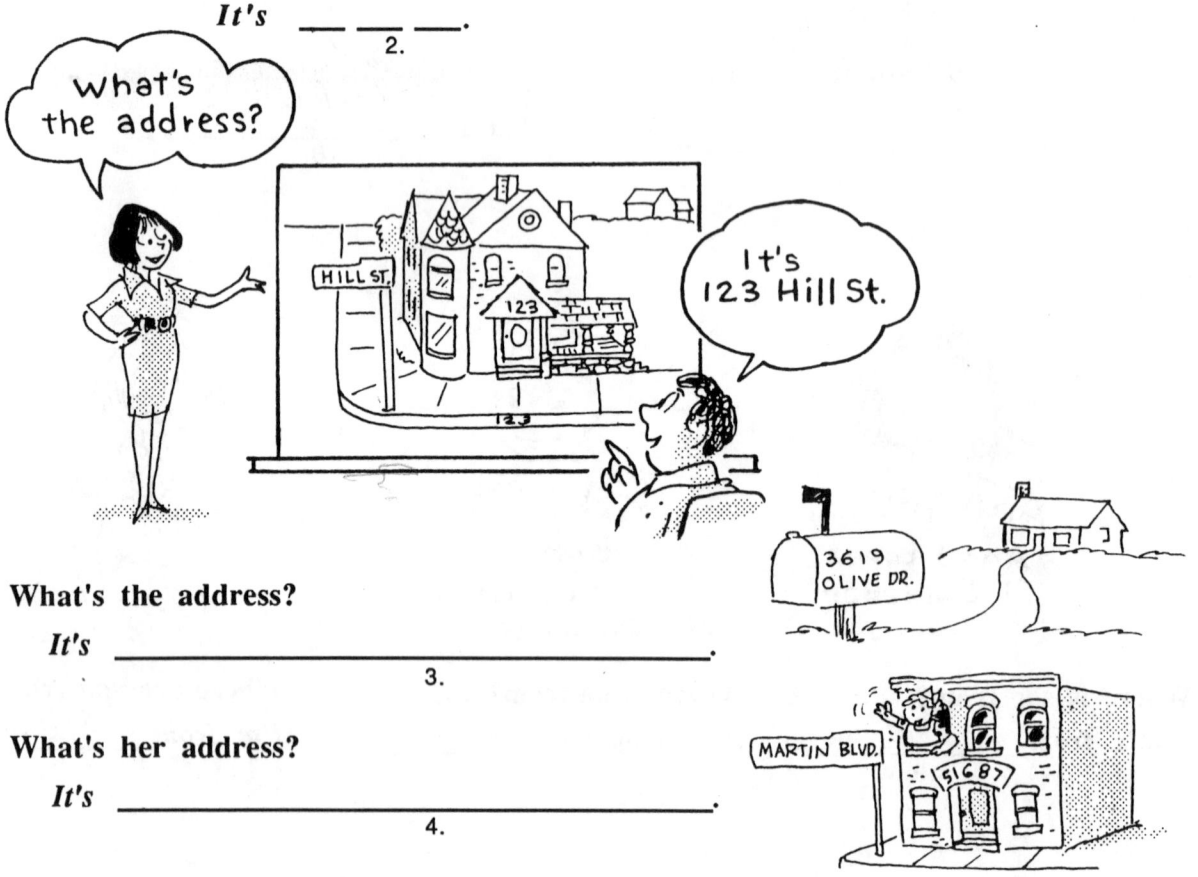

What's the address?

It's _____.
              3.

What's her address?

It's _____.
              4.

Answers: 1. (your telephone number) 2. (your area code) 3. 3619 Olive Dr. 4. 51687 Martin Blvd.

6

Making Friends

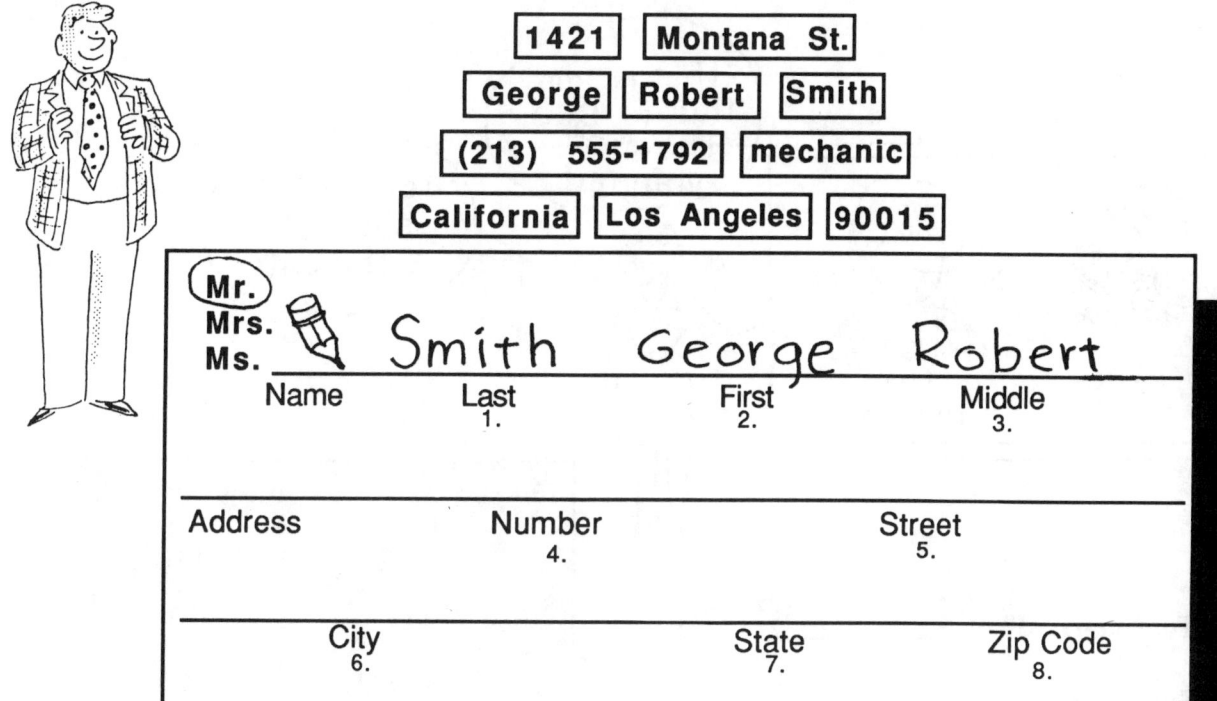

1421	Montana St.
George	Robert	Smith
(213) 555-1792	mechanic
California	Los Angeles	90015

Mr.
Mrs.
Ms. Smith   George   Robert
Name   Last   First   Middle
        1.   2.   3.

Address   Number   Street
                 4.   5.

         City   State   Zip Code
          6.   7.   8.

              Phone   Occupation
                9.   10.

What's your name?

What's your name?
   My name's _____.
                                11.

What's your address?
   It's _____.
                        12.

What's your telephone number?
   It's _____.
                        13.

What's your occupation?
   I'm a _____.
                         14.

My name's George.

Answers: 1. Smith   2. George   3. Robert   4. 1421   5. Montana St.   6. Los Angeles   7. California   8. 90015   9. (213)555-1792   10. mechanic   11. George   12. 1421 Montana St.   13. (213)555-1792   14. mechanic

7

Lesson 1d

Objective: talk about your family

Is Tom married? Yes, he is.
                 1.
Is Sue married? _____
                 2.
Are you married? _____
                 3.

Yes, I am.   No, I'm not.
he }   he }
she } is.   she } isn't.
they are.   they aren't.

Bill is the son   .
             4.
Mary is the _____.
             5.
Sue is the _____.
             6.
Tom is the _____.
             7.

Answers: 1. Yes, he is.   2. Yes, she is.   3. Yes, I am. (or) No, I'm not.   4. son   5. daughter
          6. mother   7. father

8

Making Friends

She's the wife. She's the mother. — Sue
He's the husband. He's the father. — Tom
She's the daughter. She's the sister. — Mary
He's the son. He's the brother. — Bill

Tom.

Who's the father? _____ 1.
Who's the son? _____ 2.
Who's the mother? _____ 3.
Who's the daughter? _____ 4.

Who's the brother? _____ 5.
Who's the wife? _____ 6.
Who's the sister? _____ 7.
Who's the husband? _____ 8.

Do you have any children?

Yes, I do.	No, I don't.
Yes, he/she does.	No, he/she doesn't.
Yes, they do.	No, they don't.

Yes, I do. No, I don't.

Do Tom and Sue have any children? _____ 9.
Do you have any children? _____ 10.

Answers: 1. Tom 2. Bill 3. Sue 4. Mary 5. Bill 6. Sue 7. Mary 8. Tom
9. Yes, they do. 10. Yes, I do. (or) No, I don't.

9

Review 1

Anna: Hi. My name's Anna.
Sally: Hi. My name's Sally.
Anna: What's your last name?
Sally: My last name's Miller.
Anna: Glad to meet you, Sally.
Sally: Glad to meet you, too.
Anna: Where are you from?
Sally: I'm from Canada.
Anna: What's your occupation?
Sally: I'm a doctor.
Anna: Are you married?
Sally: Yes, I am.
Anna: Do you have any children?
Sally: Yes, I have a son and a daughter.
Anna: It's late. I have to go. Good-bye.
Sally: Good-bye.

Making Friends

a.

b.

c.

d.

1. teacher
2. mechanic
3. nurse
4. student
5. gardener
6. busboy
7. doctor

e.

f.

g.

David

Pat   Bobby John Ann

My name is David Lee. This is my family. My wife and I have 3 children. We have 2 sons, Bobby and John. We have one daughter. Her name is Ann. We are from Los Angeles.

Who's the husband? _____
8.
Who's the mother? _____
9.
Is Ann the sister? _____
10.
Is Pat the sister? _____
11.

Answers: 1. f   2. g   3. b   4. a   5. c   6. e   7. d   8. David   9. Pat
10. Yes, she is.   11. No, she isn't.

11

Your Notes

Unit 2

The Neighborhood

Lesson 2a

Objective: talk about the neighborhood

Answers: 1. This is my apartment. 2. This is a house. 3. This is my street. 4. This is a corner. 5. This is a block.

The Neighborhood

Is this a street?	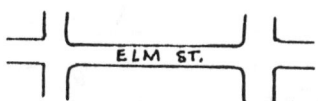	Yes, it is.
Is this a corner?		Yes, it __is__ .
		1.
Is this an apartment building?		Yes, __it__ __is__ .
		2.
Is this a street?		No, it isn't.
Is this my house?		No, __it__ __isn't__ .
		3.

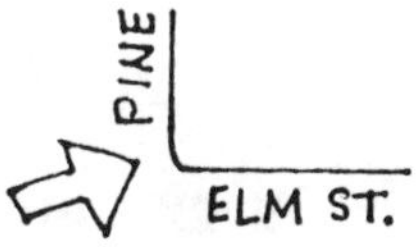

Where do you live?		in on at
I live *in* a house. an apartment. Los Angeles. *on* Elm Street. Pine Street. *at* 4311 Elm Avenue.		__on__ Pine Street 4. _____ a house 5. _____ 4311 Elm Street 6. _____ Carver Road 7. _____ 2374 Rose Avenue 8.

Answers: 1. is   2. it is   3. it isn't   4. on   5. in   6. at   7. on   8. at

15

Lesson 2b

Objectives: talk about location of places / talk about names of places

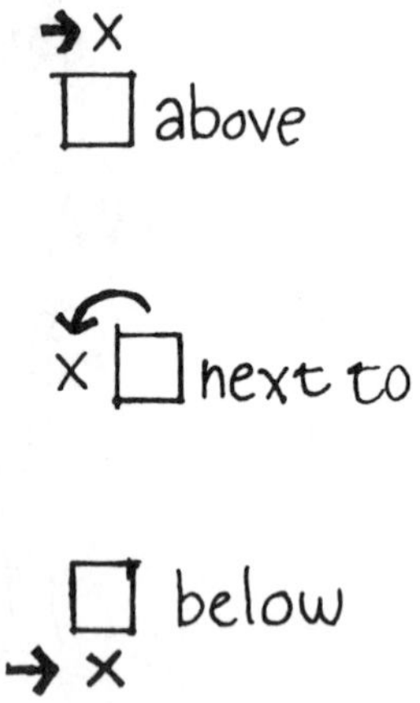

1. Their apartment is <u>above</u> my apartment.
2. His apartment is <u>next to</u> my apartment.
3. Her apartment is <u>below</u> my apartment.

What is it?

It's a park.
1.

It is a church
2.

3.

4.

5.

6.

7.

Answers: 1. It's a park. 2. It's a church. 3. It's a laundromat. 4. It's a school. 5. It's a bus stop. 6. It's a bank. 7. It's a market.

16

The Neighborhood

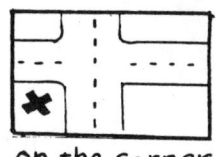
on the corner

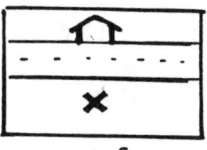
across from

next to

There is a school across from the bus stop.

There is a bank next to my building.

There is a park next to my building.

There is a church on the corner.

There is a market across from the church.

There is a church on the corner.
1.

There is a park next to my building
2.

there is a bus stop on the corner
3.

Answers: 1. There is a church on the corner. 2. There is a park next to my building.
3. There is a bus stop on the corner.

17

Lesson 2c

Objectives: talk about location of places / describe people and places

Is there a market on the corner?		Yes, __there__ __is__. 1.
Is there a laundromat across from the bank?	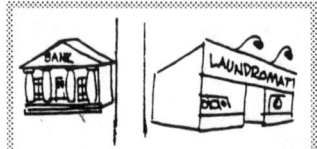	Yes, __there__ __is__. 2.
Is there a market across from the school?		No, __there__ __isn't__. 3.
Is there a bus stop across from the church?		No, __there__ __isn't__. 4.

Answers: 1. there is   2. there is   3. there isn't   4. there isn't

The Neighborhood

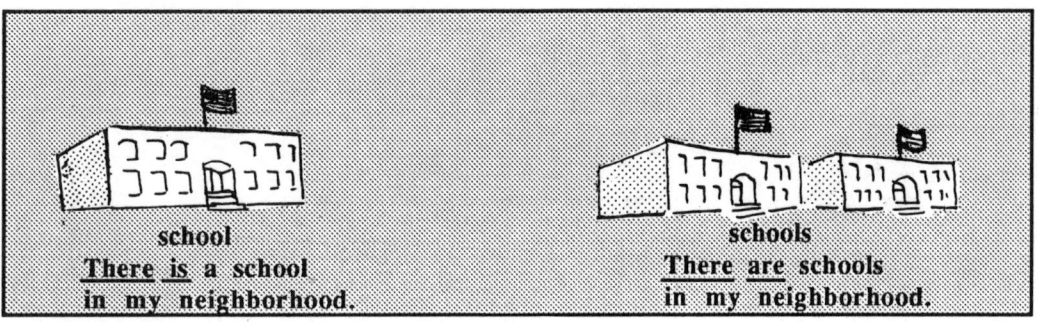

school
There **is** a school
in my neighborhood.

schools
There **are** schools
in my neighborhood.

Are there schools
in my neighborhood?   Yes, _there_ _are_ .
1.

Are there trees
in the park?   Yes, _there_ _are_ .
2.

Are there banks
in my neighborhood?   No, _there_ _aren't_ .
3.

Are there bus stops
in the park?   No, _there_ _isn't_ .
4.

"My hands are clean."

My street is _clean_.   My street is _dirty_.

"My hands are dirty."

My neighbors are _friendly_.

My neighbors are _unfriendly_.

My neighbors are _quiet_.

My neighbors are _noisy_.

Answers: 1. there are   2. there are   3. there aren't   4. there aren't

19

Lesson 2d

Objectives: ask and give directions / talk about what you can buy

Where is the laundromat?		It's __on__ Elm Street. 1.
Where is the bank?		It's __next to__ my building. 2.
Where is the park?		It's __across from__ my building. 3.
Where is the church?		It's __on__ the corner. 4.
Where is the school?		It's __on__ Pine Avenue. 5.
Where is my home?		It's __next to__ the church. 6.

Answers: 1. on   2. next to   3. across from   4. on   5. on   6. next to

20

The Neighborhood

outside the market

inside the market

What can you buy in a market?

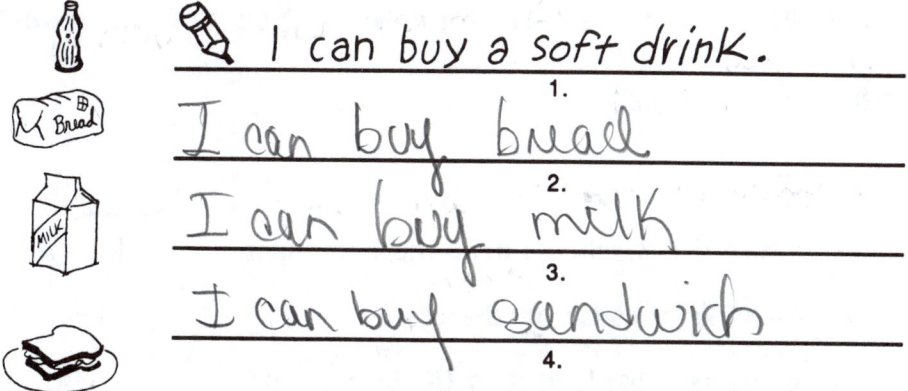

I can buy a soft drink.
1.
I can buy bread
2.
I can buy milk
3.
I can buy sandwich
4.

Answers: 1. I can buy a soft drink.   2. I can buy bread.   3. I can buy milk.   4. I can buy a sandwich.

21

Review 2

Roberto:	Hi, Sally!
Sally:	Hi, Roberto. Where do you live?
Roberto:	I live in this apartment building.
Sally:	Are there schools in this neighborhood?
Roberto:	Yes. There are 2 schools near my apartment.
Sally:	Is there a church near here?
Roberto:	Yes. There's a church on the corner.
Sally:	Where is a good market?
Roberto:	There's a good market next to the laundromat.
Sally:	Oh. There's my bus. See you in school. Good-bye.
Roberto:	Bye.

1. There are 2 schools near the apartment.   (Yes)   No
2. There is a house on the corner.   Yes   (No)
3. There is a bank next to the laundromat.   Yes   (No)
4. There is a church on the corner.   (Yes)   No

Answers: 1. Yes   2. No   3. No   4. Yes

The Neighborhood

Roberto lives on Pine Avenue in Los Angeles. The neighbors are friendly, and the street is clean. He likes the neighborhood because there is a park next to his apartment building and a bus stop on the corner. There is a good market on his block also. He can buy bread and milk at the market.

A. Roberto lives on __Pine Avenue__ in __Los Angeles__
B. The neighbors are __friendly__.
C. The __street__ is clean.
D. There is a __park__ next to his apartment building.
E. He can buy __bread__ and __milk__ at the market.

| above | next to | below |

F. The milk is __Above__ the soda.
G. The soda is __next to__ the bread.
H. The sandwich is __below__ the soda.

Answers: 1. Pine Avenue 2. Los Angeles 3. friendly 4. street 5. park 6. bread 7. milk
8. above 9. next to 10. below

Your Notes

Unit 3

Health Care

Lesson 3a

Objective — tell someone you're sick

Answers: 1. His head hurts. 2. His foot hurts. 3. His ear hurts. 4. His back hurts.

26

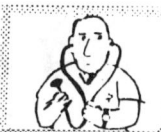

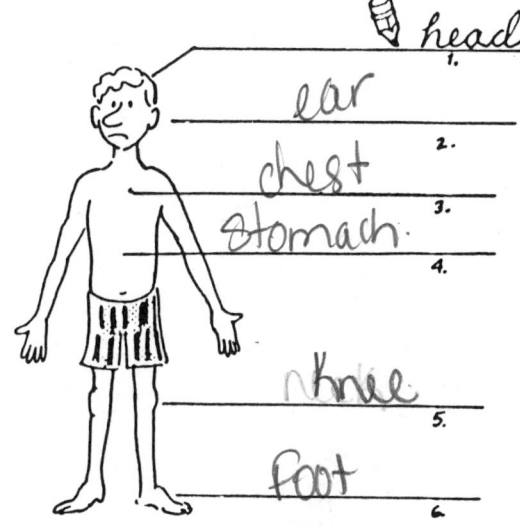

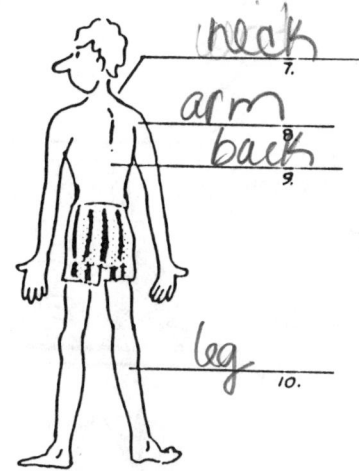

What's the matter?

My / *His*	}	*head hurts.* / *stomach hurts.*
I have / *He has*	}	*a headache* / *a stomachache.* / *an earache.* / *a toothache.* / *a backache.*

He has a stomachache.

11.

He has a Toothache.

12.

He has an earache.

13.

He has a backache.

14.

He has a headache.

15.

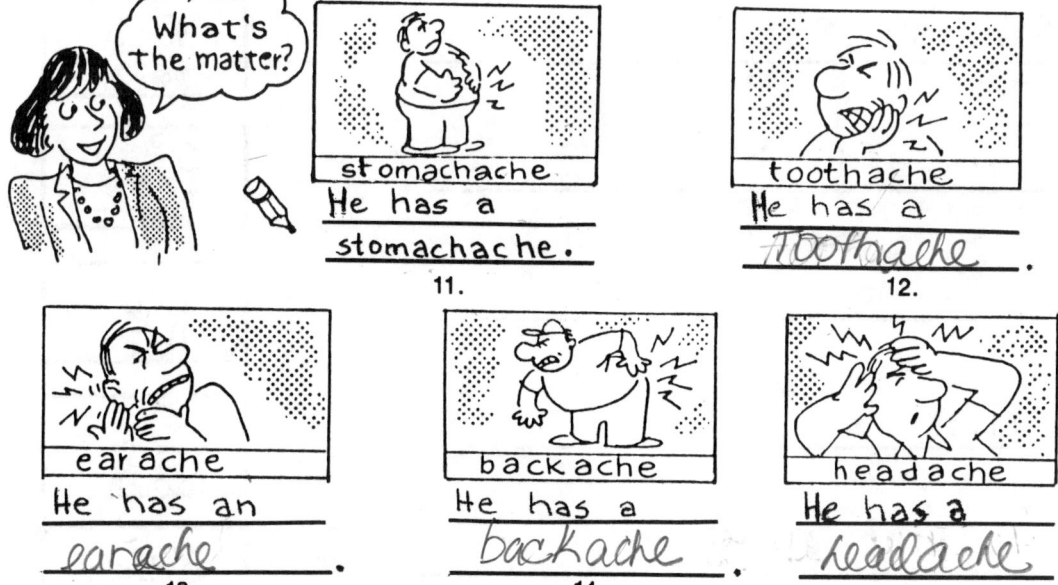

Answers: 1. head 2. ear 3. chest 4. stomach 5. knee 6. foot 7. neck 8. shoulder 9. back 10. leg 11. stomachache 12. toothache 13. earache 14. backache 15. headache

Lesson 3b

Objective: tell someone you're sick / call in sick

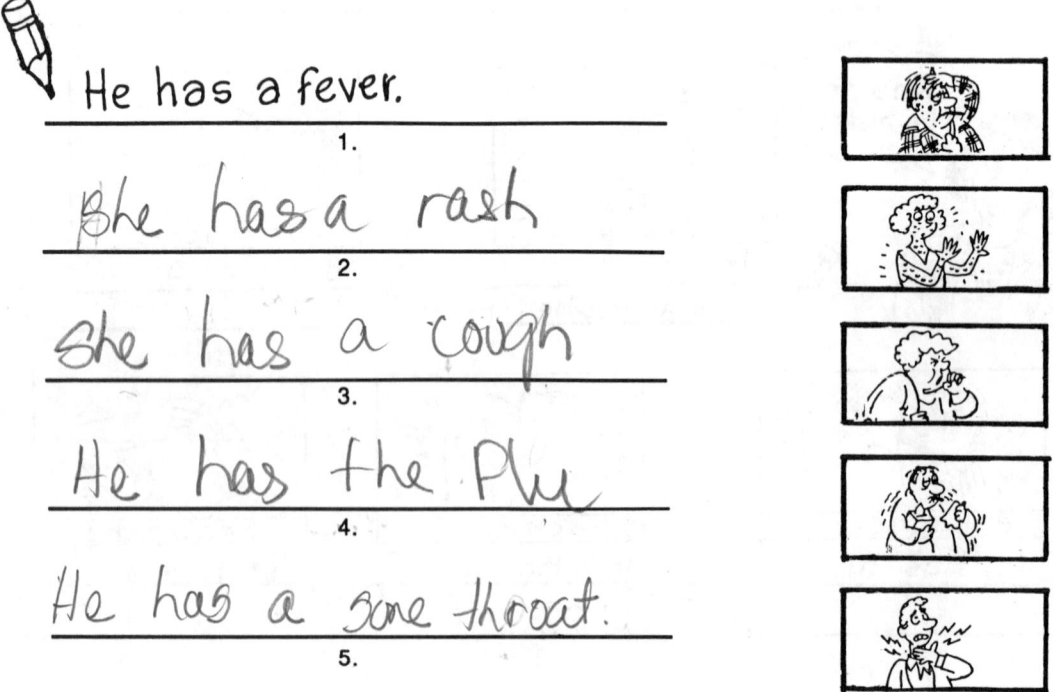

Answers: 1. He has a fever. 2. She has a rash. 3. She has a cough. 4. He has the flu. 5. He has a sore throat.

28

Health Care

Jack Miller has the flu. He's going to call in sick.

Mr. Jones: Hello. Mr. Jones speaking.
Jack: Hi, Mr. Jones. This is Jack Miller.
Mr. Jones: Hi, Jack. What's the matter?
Jack: I can't go to work. I have the flu.
Mr. Jones: Oh. That's too bad.
I hope you feel better soon.
Jack: Thanks. Good-bye.
Mr. Jones: Good-bye.

Mr. Jones: Mr. Jones speaking.
You: Hi, Mr. Jones. This is _____. 1.
Mr. Jones: What's the ___matter___? 2.
You: I can't ___go___ to work. I ___have___ the flu. 3. 4.
Mr. Jones: Oh. That's too ___bad___. 5.
I ___hope___ you ___feel___ better soon. 6. 7.
You: ___Thanks___. Good-bye. 8.
Mr. Jones: ___Good-bye___. 9.

Answers: 1. (your name) 2. matter 3. go 4. have 5. bad 6. hope 7. feel 8. Thanks 9. Good-bye

29

Lesson 3c

Objective | make a doctor's appointment

Mary Johnson works Monday, Tuesday, Wednesday and Thursday from 8 to 11.

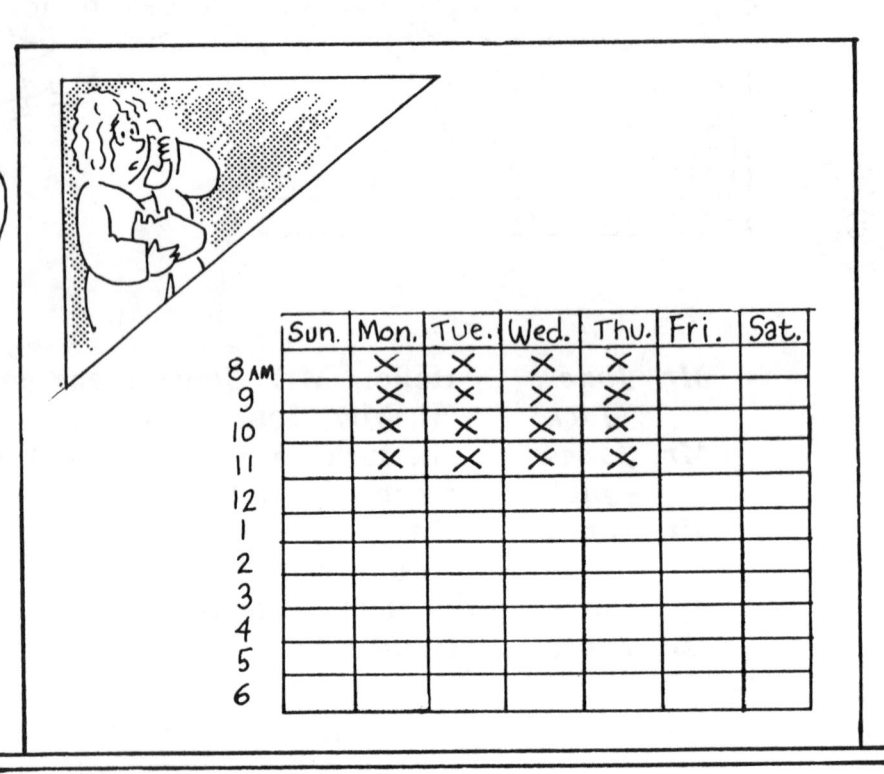

	Sun.	Mon.	Tue.	Wed.	Thu.	Fri.	Sat.
8 AM		X	X	X	X		
9		X	X	X	X		
10		X	X	X	X		
11		X	X	X	X		
12							
1							
2							
3							
4							
5							
6							

Sunday	Sunday	Sun.	Sun.	8.
Monday	Monday 2.	Mon.	Mon. 9.
Tuesday	Tuesday 3.	Tue.	Tue. 10.
Wednesday	Wednesday 4.	Wed.	Wed. 11.
Thursday	thursday 5.	Thu.	Thu. 12.
Friday	Friday 6.	Fri.	Fri. 13.
Saturday	Saturday 7.	Sat.	Sat. 14.

Answers: 1. Sunday 2. Monday 3. Tuesday 4. Wednesday 5. Thursday 6. Friday 7. Saturday. 8. Sun.
9. Mon. 10. Tue. 11. Wed. 12. Thu. 13. Fri. 14. Sat.

Health Care

Her arm hurts. She wants to see the doctor. She calls his office.

Receptionist: Hello. Doctor's office.
Mary Johnson: Hello. This is Mary Johnson.
I need to see the doctor.
Receptionist: What's the matter?
Mary Johnson: My arm hurts.
Receptionist: How about Tuesday at 9 o'clock?
Mary Johnson: No, I can't.
How about Tuesday at 3:00?
Receptionist: That's fine. Good-bye.
Mary Johnson: Good-bye.

Receptionist: Hello. Doctor's __office__.
You: Hello. This is __reyani__.
I __need__ to __see__ the doctor.
Receptionist: __What__ the matter?
You: My arm __hurts__.
Receptionist: How about __tuesday__ at 9 __o'clock__.
You: No, I __can't__.
How about Tuesday __at__ 3 o'clock.
Receptionist: That's __fine__. Good-bye.
You: __Good-bye__.

Answers: 1. office   2. (your name)   3. need   4. see   5. What's   6. hurts   7. Tuesday
8. o'clock   9. can't   10. at   11. fine   12. Good-bye

31

Lesson 3d

Objective: read medicine labels

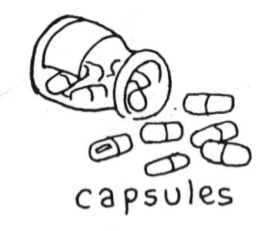

"This is Tom Smith. He has the flu."

"The doctor gives him a prescription."

"He takes the prescription to the pharmacist."

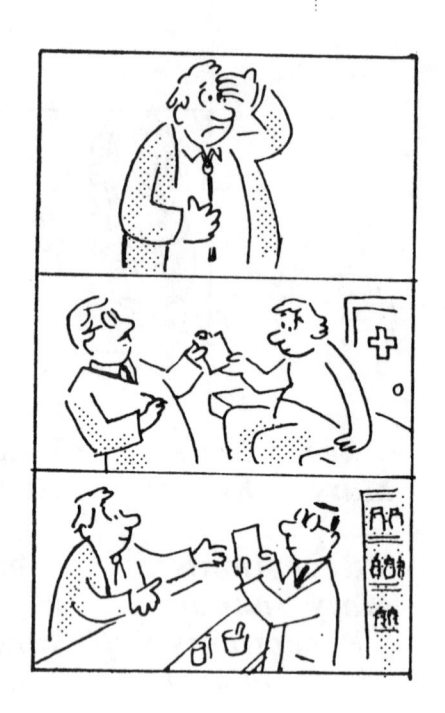

Medi-Drugs
4068 Eighth Ave
NO 478,201   555-8193
—— Dr. Lincoln ——
Tom Smith
Take 1 capsule before meals and at bedtime.

capsules

meals

bedtime

How many capsules does Tom take? __1__
1.

When does Tom take it?
before meal and at bedtime
2.

Answers: 1. 1   2. before meals and at bedtime

32

Health Care

Drug Mart
3056 Clairmont Drive
NO 556,120   555-2130
Dr. Tom Bond
Lori Howard
Take 2 teaspoons every 4 hours for cough.

I have a cough.

1 teaspoon

every 4 hours

How many teaspoons do I take? __2__
How often do I take them? __every 4 hours__

My ear hurts.

Long's Drugs
953 5th St.
NO.563,122,321   555-4191
Dr. Mary White
Sook Hee
1 drop in ear 3 times a day.

1 drop

morning   afternoon   night

How many drops does Sook take? __1__
How many times a day? __3 times a day__

Answers: 1. 2   2. every four hours   3. 1   4. 3 times

Review 3

Jack Miller can't go to work. He has a stomachache and a fever. His head hurts, too. He calls his boss at work. He also calls the doctor. The doctor gives him a prescription. Jack buys the medicine at the pharmacy. He takes 2 capsules before meals and at bedtime.

1.	Jack Miller has a sore throat.	Yes	**No**
2.	Jack Miller calls the doctor.	**Yes**	No
3.	His neck hurts.	Yes	**No**
4.	He has a stomachache.	**Yes**	No
5.	The doctor gives Jack a prescription.	**Yes**	No
6.	Jack takes 1 drop two times a day.	Yes	**No**

Answers: 1. No 2. Yes 3. No 4. Yes 5. Yes 6. No

34

Health Care

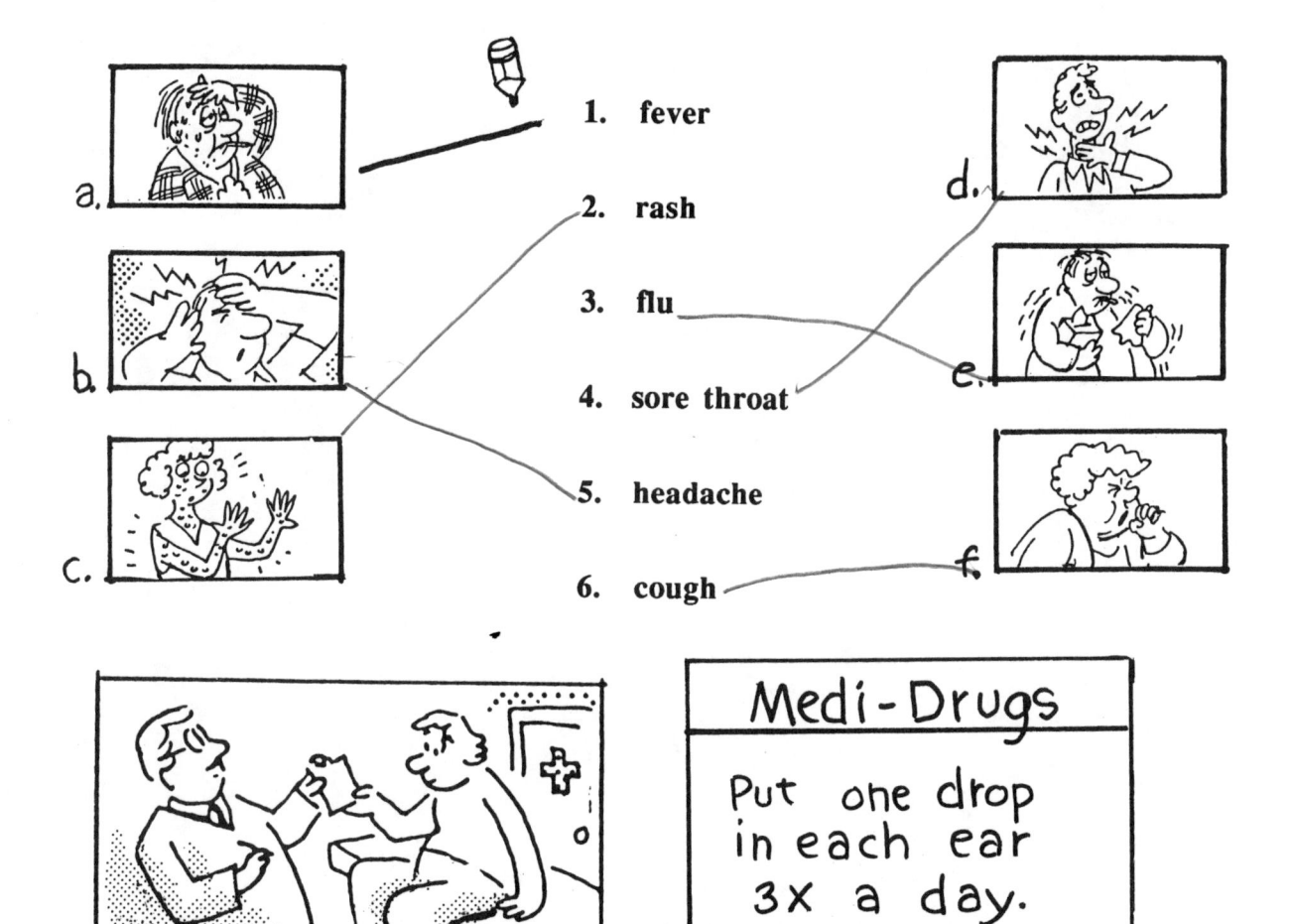

1. fever
2. rash
3. flu
4. sore throat
5. headache
6. cough

Medi-Drugs

Put one drop in each ear 3x a day.

Tom Smith has an __earache__. The doctor gives
him a __prescription__. He takes the prescription
to the __farmacist__. He puts one __drop__ in
each __ear__ 3 times a __day__.

Answers: 1. a 2. c 3. e 4. d 5. b 6. f 7. earache 8. prescription 9. pharmacist 10. drop 11. ear 12. day

35

Your Notes

Unit 4

buscando vivienda

Looking for Housing

Lesson 4a

Objectives describe an apartment
talk about problems in an apartment

This is the Sanchez family.

They live in a 3 room apartment.

bedroom | bathroom | living room | kitchen

What is it?

1. It's a bedroom.
2. It's a living room.
3. It's a Kitchen
4. It's a bathroom.

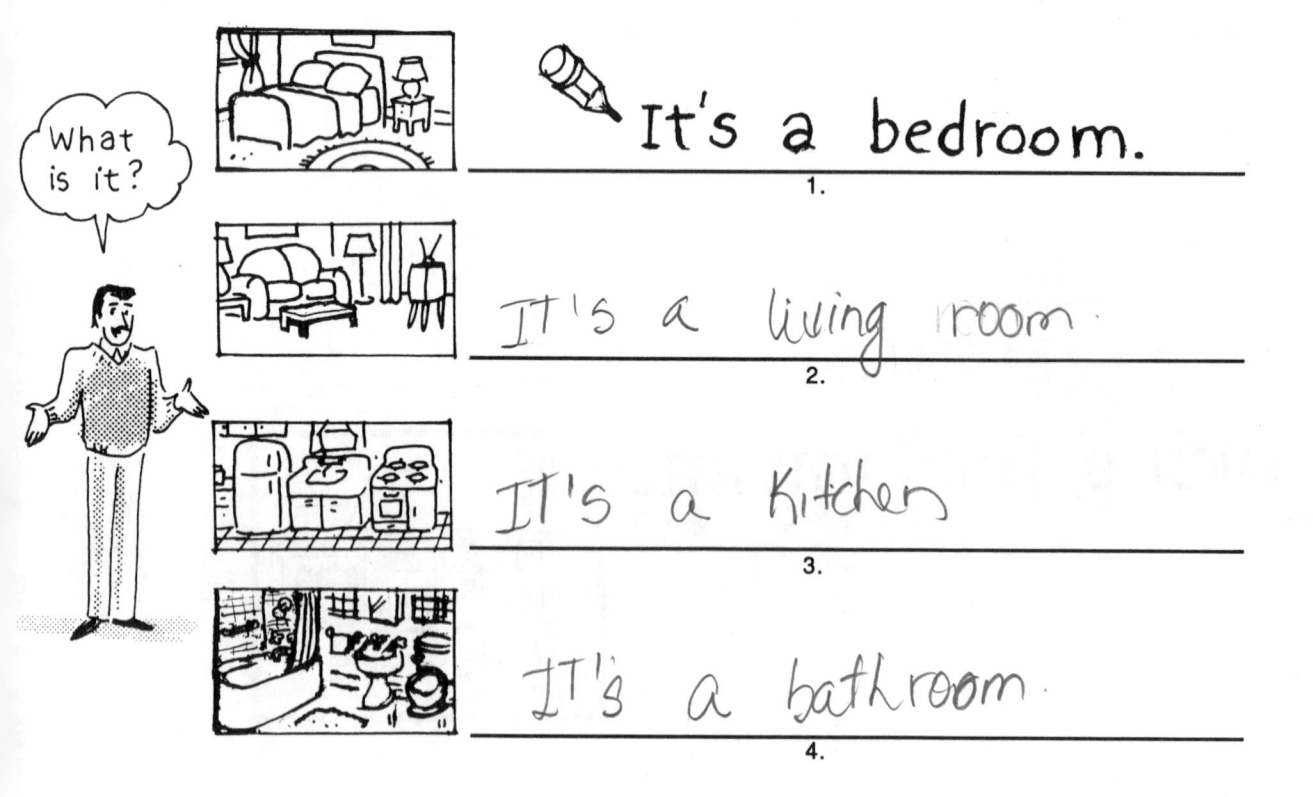

Answers: 1. It's a bedroom. 2. It's a living room. 3. It's a kitchen. 4. It's a bathroom.

38

Looking for Housing

What's the matter with the apartment?

The shower leaks.

The window is broken.

The faucet drips.

The wall is cracked.

1. What's the matter with the window?   a. It leaks.
2. What's the matter with the shower?   b. It drips.
3. What's the matter with the faucet?   c. It's cracked.
4. What's the matter with the wall?   d. It's broken.

The Sanchez family is not happy with the apartment. The window is broken. The shower leaks. The faucet drips and the wall is cracked.

They don't like the apartment. They want to move to a house.

Answers: 1. d 2. a 3. b 4. c

39

Lesson 4b

Objectives talk about more problems in an apartment
talk about looking for a house

"What are these?"

telephone
curtains
closet
carpet
locks
windows

"There are more problems in the apartment."

There isn't a telephone.
There's no _telephone_.
1.

There are no _curtains_.
4.

There isn't a closet.
There's no _closet_.
2.

There are no _locks_.
5.

There isn't a carpet.
There's no _carpet_.
3.

There are no _windows_.
6.

Answers: 1. telephone 2. closet 3. carpet 4. curtains 5. locks 6. windows

40

Looking for Housing

Buscando vivienda
alojamiento

> There *is* no } telephone. closet. carpet.
>
> There *are* no } curtains. locks. windows.

1. There __is__ no telephone.
2. There __are__ no curtains.
3. There __is__ no carpet.
4. There __are__ no locks.
5. There __is__ no closet.
6. There __are__ no windows.

There are many problems in the Sanchez apartment. They want to live in a house with no problems. They want a house with 3 bedrooms.

How can they find a house? They can ask their friends. They can also look in the newspaper and look around their neighborhood.

Answers: 1. is 2. are 3. is 4. are 5. is 6. are

Lesson 4c

Objective — talk about looking for a house

The Sanchez family wants a 3 bedroom house with a yard and a garage.

BR = bedroom   BA = bathroom   Apt. = apartment
2+2 = 2 bedrooms and 2 bathrooms

FOR RENT
House, 2 BR, 1 BA
$450 / month

How many bedrooms? __2__
How many bathrooms? __1__
How much is the rent? __$450__

How many bedrooms? __2__
How many bathrooms? __2__
How much is the rent? __$425__

FOR RENT
APT, 2 + 2
$425 / month

FOR RENT
House, 2 BR, 2 BA
$475 / month

How many bedrooms? __2__
How many bathrooms? __2__
How much is the rent? __$475__

Answers: 1. 2   2. 1   3. $450 / month   4. 2   5. 2   6. $425 / month   7. 2   8. 2   9. $475 / month

42

Looking for Housing

This is a good house for the Sanchez family.

How many bedrooms are there? __3__
1.
How many bathrooms are there? __2__
2.
How much is the rent? __450__
3.

__D__ dining room
4.
__C__ living room
5.
____ bathroom
6.
__F__ garage
7.
__A__ yard
8.
__E__ kitchen
9.

Answers: 1. 3 2. 2 3. $450/month 4. D 5. C 6. B 7. F 8. A 9. E

43

Lesson 4d

Objectives: describe a house / describe a neighborhood

The Sanchez family likes their new house because there are no problems.

Why do they like this house?

Because there are no dripping faucets.

Because there are no cracked walls.

Because there are no broken windows.

Why do they like this house?

Because there are many windows.

1. Because there is a yard.
2. Because there is a telephone.
3. Because there is a garage.
4. Because there are locks.

Answers: 1. Because there is a yard. 2. Because there is a telephone. 3. Because there is a garage. 4. Because there are locks.

Looking for Housing

Why do they like this neighborhood?

Because there is a ___school___ next to the house
1.

Because there is a ___church___ near the house.
2.

Because there is a ___bus stop___ on the corner.
3.

The Sanchez family lives in a big house near a school. There are 3 bedrooms in the house. They have a small yard and a garage. They like their new house.

Answers: 1. school   2. church   3. bus stop

Review 4

The Sanchez family lives in an apartment with many problems. A window is broken, the shower leaks and the wall is cracked. There are no curtains or locks. There isn't a carpet. They want to move to a house with 3 bedrooms, a yard and a garage. They want to live near a school. They ask their friends and look in the newspaper to find a new house.

1. The apartment has a carpet.   Yes   (No)
2. A window is broken.   Yes   No
3. The Sanchez family wants a new house.   Yes   No
4. They want to live near a bank.   Yes   No
5. They want a house with 1 bedroom.   Yes   No
6. They look in the newspaper to find a house.   Yes   No

Answers: 1. No 2. Yes 3. Yes 4. No 5. No 6. Yes

Looking for Housing

a.

b.

c.

d.

1. curtains
2. locks
3. telephone
4. carpet
5. closet
6. windows
7. shower
8. wall

e.

f.

g.

h.

| is | are |

9. There ___are___ no curtains.
10. There _____ no telephone.
11. There _____ a yard.
12. There _____ a garage.
13. There _____ locks.
14. There _____ many windows.
15. There _____ a carpet.
16. There _____ no closets.

Answers: 1. a 2. h 3. c 4. b 5. e 6. g 7. d 8. f 9. are 10. is 11. is 12. is
13. are 14. are 15. is 16. are

47

Your Notes

Unit 5

Marketing

Lesson 5a

Objective | talk about groceries

Fred bought these at the market.

FRED   ROVER

lettuce   an apple   a soft drink
milk   a banana   coffee
sugar   a cookie   rice

What do you have?

I have _____.
1.

I have _____ _____.
2.

I have _____.
3.

50   Answers: 1. a soft drink   2. sugar and milk   3. lettuce

Marketing

"Fred bought 2 apples. He bought 3 bananas."

"He bought lettuce, too."

an apple — 2 apples
a banana — 3 bananas
a soft drink — 2 soft drinks
a cookie — 5 cookies

COUNT

lettuce   rice
milk   sugar
coffee   dog food

NON-COUNT

What does Fred have?

1. Fred has __cereal__.
2. He has _____. 
3. He has _____. 
4. He has _____. 

What does Fred need?

5. Fred needs _____.
6. He needs _____. 
7. He needs _____. 
8. He needs _____. 

Answers: 1. cereal   2. rice   3. coffee   4. sugar   5. lettuce   6. milk   7. dog food   8. bananas

51

Lesson 5b

Objective: ask for information in a market

Fred is in the supermarket.

is

1. Where __is__ the lettuce?
2. Where _____ the milk?
3. Where _____ the dog food?
4. Where _____ the rice?

are

5. Where _____ the bananas?
6. Where _____ the apples?
7. Where _____ the cookies?
8. Where _____ the soft drinks?

the dairy section   the produce section   the bakery section   aisle 5

Where _____ the lettuce?   In the _____ section.
         9.   10.
Where _____ the cookies?   In the _____ section.
         11.   12.
Where _____ the milk?   In the _____ section.
         13.   14.
Where _____ the soft drinks?   On _____ 5.
         15.   16.

Answers: 1. is 2. is 3. is 4. is 5. are 6. are 7. are 8. are 9. is 10. produce
11. are 12. bakery 13. is 14. dairy 15. are 16. aisle

52

Marketing

Fred: Excuse me. Where are the soft drinks?
Lady: On aisle 5.
Fred: Are the cookies on aisle 5, too?
Lady: No, the cookies are in the bakery section.
Fred: And where is the milk?
Lady: In the dairy section.
Fred: Thank you.

Fred: Excuse me. Where are the __soft__ __drinks__?
   1.
Lady: On _____ 5.
          2.
Fred: Are the _____ on aisle 5, too?
              3.
Lady: No, the cookies are in the _____ section.
                                    4.
Fred: And where is the _____ ?
                          5.
Lady: In the _____ section.
              6.
Fred: Thank you.

Answers: 1. soft drinks 2. aisle 3. cookies 4. bakery 5. milk 6. dairy

Lesson 5c

Objective: talk more about groceries

This is a can of dog food.

- a can of dog food
- 2 cans of dog food
- an ear of corn
- 2 ears of corn
- a head of lettuce
- a loaf of bread
- a carton of milk

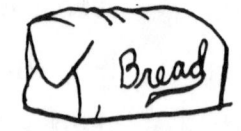

1. a carton of
2. 2 cans of
3. a loaf of
4. a head of
5. 2 ears of

a.
b.
c.
d.
e.

Answers: 1. b 2. c 3. d 4. a 5 e

54

Marketing

Do you have some corn?

No, I don't have any corn. I have some cookies.

No, I don't have any corn. I have some rice.

No, I don't have any corn. I have some apples.

| some | any |

1. I have __some__ lettuce.

2. I have _____ milk.

3. I don't have _____ coffee.

4. I have _____ dog food.

5. I don't have _____ bread.

6. I have _____ corn.

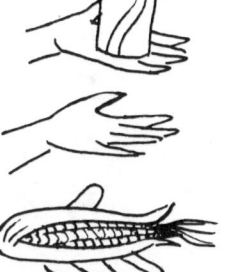

Answers: 1. some   2. some   3. any   4. some   5. any   6. some

55

Lesson 5d

Objective: ask for things in a market

Fred is at the counter. The lady will help him.

Lady:	May I help you?
Fred:	Not yet. I'm still looking.
Lady:	OK.
Fred:	What's this?
Lady:	That's potato salad.
Fred:	What's that?
Lady:	That's apple salad.
Fred:	It looks good. I'd like enough for one person.
Lady:	Here you are.
Fred:	Thanks a lot.

Marketing

Lady: May I __help__ you?
                1.
Fred: Not _____. I'm _____ looking.
             2.   3.
Lady: OK.
Fred: What's _____?
                  4.
Lady: That's potato _____.
                          5.
Fred: What's _____?
                  6.
Lady: That's _____ salad.
                   7.
Fred: It _____ good. I'd like _____
            8.   9.
for one _____.
              10.
Lady: Here _____.
              11.
Fred: Thanks ____ _____.
                    12.

Answers: 1. help 2. yet 3. still 4. this 5. salad 6. that 7. apple 8. looks
9. enough 10. person 11. you are 12. a lot

57

Review 5

When I need groceries, I go to the supermarket. The apples and bananas are in the produce section. The cookies are in the bakery section. The coffee is on aisle 3, and the rice is on aisle 5. The lady helps me at the deli counter. The apple salad looks good.

I have some groceries in my shopping cart. I have 4 ears of corn, a head of lettuce, a carton of milk and some cereal. I also have 3 cans of dog food for Rover. I don't need any bread because I have a loaf of bread at home. I have enough groceries now.

1. Fred has 4 ears of corn in his shopping cart.   (Yes)   No
2. He has 2 heads of lettuce in his shopping cart.   Yes   No
3. He has some cereal in his shopping cart.   Yes   No
4. He needs some bread.   Yes   No

Answers: 1. Yes   2. No   3. Yes   4. No

Marketing

Where are the cookies? Where is the milk?

1. cookies

2. milk

3. corn

4. bread

5. lettuce

6. apple salad

7. bananas

8. potato salad

9. apples

a. the dairy section

b. the produce section

c. the bakery section

d. the deli section

Answers: 1. c   2. a   3. b   4. c   5. b   6. d   7. b   8. d   9. b

59

Your Notes

Unit 6

Recreation and Leisure

Lesson 6a

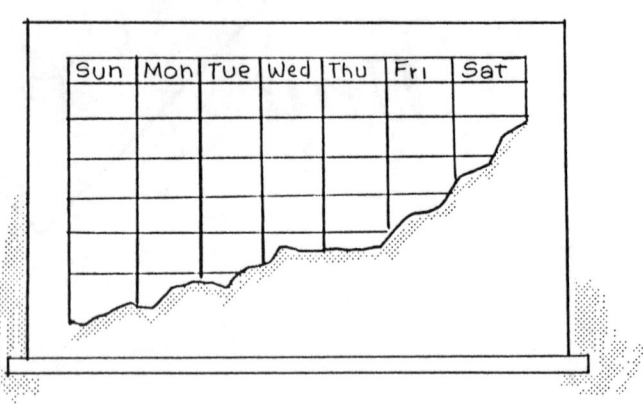

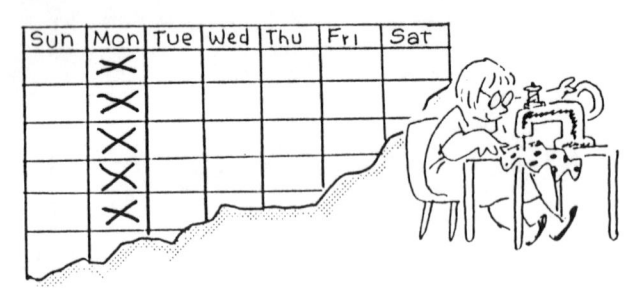

Objective describe daily activities

"These are the days of the week."

What does Sara do every Monday?
She works.

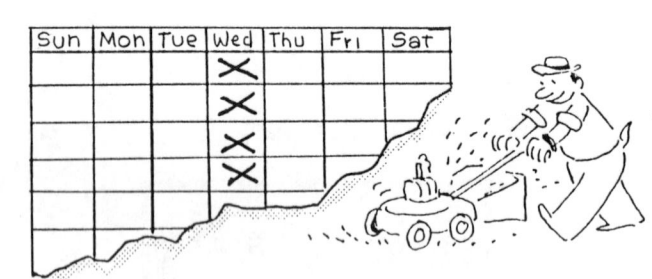

What does Joe do every Tuesday?
He ____works____.
　　　　1.

What does he do every Wednesday?
He _____.
　　　　2.

What does he do every Thursday?
He _____.
　　　　3.

Answers: 1. works 2. works 3. works

62

Recreation and Leisure

She works _____ through _____.
             1.   2.
She _____ 5 days a week.
       3.

What do {you, they} do?   I, They } work.

What does {he, she} do?   He, She } works.

What do you do?   ___I___ work.
                             4.
What does he do?   _____ works.
                             5.
What do they do?   _____ _____
                                    6.
What does she do?   _____ _____
                                    7.

Answers: 1. Monday   2. Friday   3. works   4. I   5. He   6. They work.   7. She works.

63

Lesson 6b

Objectives: describe what people do at work
describe what people do after work

"What's her occupation?"
"What does she do?"

"She's a seamstress."
"She sews."

He's a mechanic.
He fixes cars.

He's a gardener.
He cuts the grass.

He's a busboy.
He cleans tables.

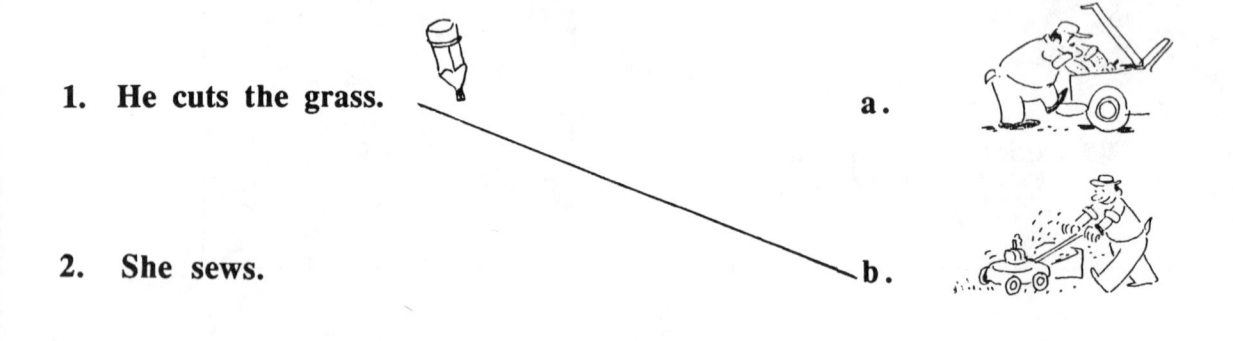

1. He cuts the grass. a.

2. She sews. b.

3. He cleans the tables. c.

4. He fixes cars. d.

Answers: 1. b 2. c 3. d 4. a

64

Recreation and Leisure

"What **does** she do after work?"

She rests.

"What **do** they do after work?"

They eat dinner.

She rests.

He listens to music.

They eat dinner.

They watch T.V.

What ___do___ they do after work?
        1.

They _____ dinner.
     2.

What _____ she do after work?
         3.

She _____.
      4.

What _____ they do after work?
         5.

They _____.
      6.

Answers: 1. do 2. eat 3. does 4. rests 5. do 6. read

65

Lesson 6c Objective: talk about what's happening now

What's he doing now? — He is resting.

What is she doing now?
She __is__ reading.
1.

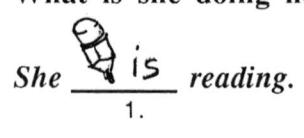

What is he doing now?
He _____ listening to music.
2.

What is she doing now?
She _____ watching TV.
3.

What are you doing now?
- I am listening to the radio.
- I am cleaning.
- I am drinking.

Answers: 1. is 2. is 3. is

66

Recreation and Leisure

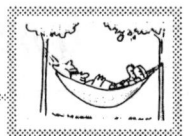

Sara works Monday through Friday. Saturday is her day off.

What are you doing?	I am drinking.
What is he/she doing?	He/She is reading.
What are they doing?	They are resting.

It's his day off.
What is he doing?

He __is__ playing soccer.
1.

It's their day off.
What are they doing?

They _____ watching baseball.
2.

What are you doing now?

I _____ learning English.
3.

Answers: 1. is 2. are 3. am

67

Lesson 6d

Objectives: talk about months, seasons, weather and sports

"What are the seasons?"

Seasons	Months		
winter	January	February	March
spring	April	May	June
summer	July	August	September
fall	October	November	December

"The seasons are winter, spring, summer, fall."

rainy
hot
sunny
cold
windy

"How is the weather?"

How is the weather?

It's __rainy__.
1.

It's _____.
2.

It's _____.
3.

It's _____.
4.

It's _____.
5.

rainy
sunny
cold
windy
hot

Answers: 1. rainy 2. sunny 3. cold 4. windy 5. hot

Recreation and Leisure

"What are they doing now?"

They are skiing.

They are playing soccer.

They are playing basketball.

They are playing football.

They are playing baseball.

She is swimming.

"They ski."

"What do they do in the winter?"

What does he do in the fall?

He plays __football__.
1.

What do they do in the winter?

They play _____.
2.

What do they do in the summer?

They play _____.
3.

What do they do every season?

They play _____.
4.

Answers: 1. football 2. basketball 3. baseball 4. soccer

69

Review 6

Joe is a mechanic. He fixes cars. He works five days a week, Monday through Friday.

Joe rests after work. He listens to music, eats dinner and sometimes watches TV.

Saturdays and Sundays are his days off. In the winter Joe plays basketball. In the summer, he plays baseball. He plays soccer in the summer, too.

1. *Joe is a* __mechanic__.

2. *Joe* _____ *after work.*

3. *He* _____ *dinner.*

4. *His days off are* _____ ____ _____.

5. *He* _____ *basketball in the winter.*

Answers: 1. mechanic 2. rests 3. eats 4. Saturdays and Sundays 5. plays

Recreation and Leisure

EVERY DAY		**NOW**
She ✏ _works_ . 1.		She is ✏ _working_ . 2.
He _____ cars. 3.		He is _____ cars. 4.
He _____ to music. 5.		He is _____ to music. 6.
She _____. 7.		She is _____. 8.
They _____ dinner. 9.		They are _____ dinner. 10.

☞ What do you do every day? _____
11.

☞ What are you doing now? _____
12.

Answers: 1. works 2. working 3. fixes 4. fixing 5. listens 6. listening 7. rests
8. resting 9. eat 10. eating 11. I _____ every day. 12. I am _____-ing now.

71

Your Notes

Unit 7

Buying Clothing

Lesson 7a

Objectives: talk about clothing / talk about colors

"Tom and Sue have lots of clothes in their closet."

"Tom has a jacket. Sue has a sweater."

Tom   Sue

Tom has a pair of pants.   He has a shirt.   He has a pair of shoes.

Sue has a skirt.    She has a blouse.    She has a dress.

"What does Tom have in his closet?"

1. He has a shirt. 
2. _____ 
3. _____

"What does Sue have in her closet?"

4. _____

74

Answers: 1. He has a shirt. 2. He has a jacket. 3. She has a skirt. 4. She has a blouse.

Buying Clothing

"What color is this jacket?"

- blue
- red
- yellow
- green
- orange
- brown
- black
- white

"It's blue."

This is a skirt. It's orange.
✏️ It's an orange skirt.
1.

This is a shirt. It's white.
2. _____

This is a blouse. It's red.
3. _____

This is a sweater. It's green.
4. _____

This is a jacket. It's blue.
5. _____

This is a pair of pants. It's brown.
6. _____

Answers: 1. It's an orange shirt. 2. It's a white shirt. 3. It's a red blouse. 4. It's a green sweater. 5. It's a blue jacket. 6. It's a brown pair of pants.

Lesson 7b

Objective talk about buying clothing

Salesman: May I help you?

Tom: Yes, I need a jacket.

Salesman: How about this black one?

Tom: No, I don't like black.

Salesman: How about this brown one?

Tom: That's fine. I like brown.

Salesman: May I __help__ you?
                1.

Tom: Yes, I _____ a jacket.
               2.

Salesman: How about this _____ one?
                3.

Tom: No, I don't _____ black.
               4.

Salesman: How about this brown one?

Tom: That's fine. I like _____.
               5.

Answers: 1. help 2. need 3. black 4. like 5. brown

Buying Clothing

"How about this one?"

I don't like green.
1.
2.
3.
4.
5.
6.

"What size is this?"

S M L

"It's small." "It's medium." "It's large."

Answers: 1. I don't like green. 2. I like yellow. 3. I don't like red. 4. I like black. 5. I don't like blue. 6. I like white.

77

Lesson 7c

Objective | talk about buying clothing

"Tom needs a new jacket. He likes the brown one."

"I'd like to try it on. Where are the dressing rooms?"

"The dressing rooms are over there."

"Tom tries on the jacket."

"How does it fit?"

"It's too large."

1. small — It's too small.
2. tight — _____
3. loose — _____
4. long — _____
5. short — _____

It fits fine.

78   Answers: 1. It's too small. 2. It's too tight. 3. It's too loose. 4. It's too long. 5. It's too short.

Buying Clothing

Sue wants to buy a skirt. How does it fit?

It's too large.

1. It's too small.
2.
3.
4.
5.
6.

Answers: 1. It's too small. 2. It's too tight. 3. It's too loose. 4. It's too long. 5. It's too short.
6. It fits fine.

Lesson 7d

Objective talk about exchanging clothing

Sue buys a dress for her daughter. It's too large.

She takes it back to the department store and exchanges it.

Saleswoman:	May I help you?
Sue:	Yes. I want to exchange this dress.
Saleswoman:	What's the matter?
Sue:	It's too large. I need a smaller one.

Saleswoman:	May I <u>help</u> you? 　　　　　1.
Sue:	Yes. I want to _____ this dress. 　　　　　　　　　　　2.
Saleswoman:	What's the _____ ? 　　　　　　　　3.
Sue:	It's too _____ . 　　　　　4. I need a _____ one. 　　　　　　5.

80　　　Answers: 1. help 2. exchange 3. matter 4. large 5. smaller

Buying Clothing

"Which one is larger?"

"The blue one is larger."

Which one is smaller?

The red one is smaller.
1.

Which one is larger?

_____
2.

Which one is larger?

_____
3.

the red one = the red dress

"Which one is smaller?"

"The red one."

Which one is larger?

_____
4.

Which one is smaller?

_____
5.

Which one is larger?

_____
6.

Answers: 1. The red one is smaller. 2. The yellow one is larger. 3. The red one is larger. 4. The yellow one. 5. The red one. 6. The blue one.

81

Review 7

Tom has lots of clothes in his closet. He has a green pair of pants and a brown pair of shoes. He has a blue shirt and a brown jacket. The brown jacket is old. He needs a new jacket.

He goes to the men's clothing department at the department store. The salesman helps Tom try on many jackets. Tom doesn't like the red jacket. He likes the brown one, but it's too large. He needs a smaller one. The black one is too tight. He tries on a green jacket. It's not too small, and it's not too tight. The sleeves are not too short, and they are not too long. The green jacket fits fine.

1.	Tom has a green pair of shoes.	Yes	*No*
2.	He has a red jacket.	Yes	No
3.	He needs a new jacket.	Yes	No
4.	Tom likes the red jacket.	Yes	No
5.	The black jacket is too loose.	Yes	No
6.	The green jacket fits fine.	Yes	N

Answers: 1. No   2. No   3. Yes   4. No   5. No   6.

Buying Clothing

"What does Sue have in her closet?"

1. She has a black skirt.
2. _____ 
3. _____ 
4. _____

"Sue wants to buy a skirt. How does it fit?"

a.

b.

c.

5. It's too large.

6. It's too tight.

7. It's too small.

8. It's too loose.

9. It's too short.

10. It fits fine.

d.

e.

f.

Answers: 1. She has a black skirt. 2. She has an orange sweater. 3. She has a yellow dress. 4. She has a red pair of shoes. 5. b 6. c 7. a 8. e 9. d 10. f

Your Notes

Unit 8

Getting a Job

Lesson 8a

Objective

Joe is a mechanic. He works Monday through Friday. He has a full-time job.

He doesn't have a job. He needs a job.

What's the matter?

I have	I don't have
He has	He doesn't have

I need	I don't need
He needs	He doesn't need

1. Joe ____has____ a full-time job.

2. What's the matter? There is no work for Joe. He doesn't _____ a job.

3. He _____ a job.

86   Answers: 1. has   2. have   3. needs

Getting a Job

What is Joe's job in this country?

What was his job in his country?

He is a mechanic in this country.

He was a mechanic in his country.

is   was

1. What is Sara's job in this country?

   She _____is_____ an office worker.

2. What was her job in her country?

   She _____ a secretary.

3. What is Jim's job in this country?

   He _____ a plumber.

4. What was his job in his country?

   He _____ a house painter.

5. What is Rebecca's job in this country?

   She _____ a cook.

6. What was her job in her country?

   She _____ a seamstress.

Answers: 1. is   2. was   3. is   4. was   5. is   6. was

87

Lesson 8b

Objective | talk about job skills

What can a mechanic do?

He can fix cars.

What can an office worker do?

She ___can___ file.
    1.

What can a secretary do?

He _____ type.
    2.

3. What can a plumber do?
   He can repair sinks.

4. What can a house painter do?
   He can paint.

5. What can a cook do?
   She can cook.

6. What can a seamstress do?
   She can sew.

a.

b.

c.

d.

Answers: 1. can 2. can 3. b 4. a 5. d 6. c

Getting a Job

What can a mechanic fix?
He can fix all kinds of cars.

What can a seamstress sew?
She can sew all kinds of clothes.

What can a house painter paint?
He can paint all kinds of houses.

May I help you?
I'm an office worker. I need a part-time job.
What can you do?
I can file.
Can you type, too?
Yes, I can type all kinds of letters.

May I _____help_____ you?
1.
I'm an office worker. I _____ a part-time job.
2.
What _____ you do?
3.
I can _____.
4.
Can you _____, too?
5.
Yes, I can type all _____ of letters.
6.

Answers: 1. help 2. need 3. can 4. file 5. type 6. kinds

89

Lesson 8c

Objective: read ads for jobs

These are the want ads. Rebecca and Sara can look in the ads for jobs

Classified Ads

What is necessary for Rebecca?

Experienced Waitress
M-F
7am - 3pm
Dave's Coffee Shop
7th and Westland
Apply in person

→ She must have experience.
→ She must work full time.
→ She must go to Dave's Coffee Shop.

What is necessary for Sara?

Doctor's Office Needs part-time Secretary
Bi-ling. Spanish
213/555-3674

→ She has to speak English and Spanish
→ She has to call

1. She ____must____ have experience.

2. She _____ work full-time.

3. She _____ go to Dave's coffee shop.

must = has to

4. She ____has____ ____to____ speak English and Spanish.

5. She _____ _____ call.

90   Answers: 1. must 2. must 3. must 4. has to 5. has to

Getting a Job

Sara called the doctor about a job.

Dr. Newman: Do you have any experience?
Sara: Yes. I worked in an office in Colombia.
Dr. Newman: Can you type?
Sara: Yes. I can type 70 words per minute.
Dr. Newman: That's good.

Dr. Newman: Do you have any __experience__ ?
                                    1.
Sara: Yes. I _____ in an _____ in Colombia.
                  2.   3.
Dr. Newman: Can you _____ ?
                          4.
Sara: Yes. I _____ type 70 words per minute.
                  5.
Dr. Newman: That's _____ .
                         6.

Answers: 1. experience   2. worked   3. office   4. type   5. can   6. good

91

Lesson 8d

Objectives talk about job interviews
talk about the past

Joe has to apply in person for a job. He has to see Mr. Manning.

do - did
work - worked
repair - repaired

Mr. Manning: Do you have any experience?
Joe: Yes. I was a mechanic in my country for 5 years.
Mr. Manning: Where did you work there?
Joe: I worked at Tim's Garage.
Mr. Manning: What did you do?
Joe: I repaired all kinds of cars and trucks.

Mr. Manning: Do you have any ____experience____?
1.
Joe: Yes. I _____ a _____ in my
     2.   3.
country for 5 years.
Mr. Manning: Where _____ you work there?
             4.
Joe: I _____ at Tim's Garage.
     5.
Mr. Manning: What _____ you do?
             6.
Joe: I _____ all kinds of _____ and trucks.
     7.   8.

Answers: 1. experience 2. was 3. mechanic 4. did 5. worked 6. did 7. repaired 8. cars

Getting a Job

Joe needs a job. He looks in the want ads.

Auto Mechanic
Exp'd
Good Pay
Al's Auto Repair
2346 W. Baily St.
Apply in person
Week-days
See Mr. Manning

What is necessary for Joe?

→ He must have experience.

→ He has to go to Al's Auto Repair.

→ He must see Mr. Manning.

1. (213) 555-3674
2. Bi-ling. Spanish
3. M-F 7am-3pm
4. Exp'd.

a. You must work full-time.
b. You have to call.
c. You must have experience.
d. You have to speak English and Spanish.

Answers: 1. b 2. d 3. a 4. c

93

Review 8

Joe is a mechanic. He needs a full-time job. He can fix all kinds of cars and trucks. He has many years of experience. He looks at the want ads in the newspaper for a job. Al's Auto Repair needs an experienced auto mechanic. Joe has to apply for the job in person. He must see Mr. Manning for an interview.

1. Joe is a _____mechanic_____.
2. He needs a _____-_____ job.
3. He can_____all _____of cars.
4. Joe has to apply for the job_____ _____.
5. He must see Mr. Manning for an_____.

94   Answers: 1. mechanic   2. full-time   3. fix, kinds   4. in person   5. interview

Getting a Job

1.  He can fix cars.
2. 
3. 
4. 
5.

6. Is this a full-time or part-time job?

7. Can you apply at 3 pm?

8. Do you need experience?

9. Where do you apply?

```
Cook
M - F
8 a.m. - 4 p.m.
Exp'd
Apply 2-4 p.m.
459 First St.
```

Answers: 1. He can fix cars. 2. He can cook. 3. He can type. 4. She can sew. 5. She can file. 6. Full-time. 7. Yes. 8. Yes. 9. 459 First St.

Your Notes

Unit 9

On The Job

Lesson 9a

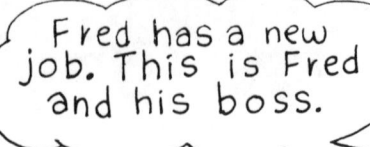

Objective — talk about the days of the week

"Fred has a new job. This is Fred and his boss."

"A schedule is the days and hours of work."

"Fred works Tuesday through Saturday. Sunday and Monday are his days off."

Sunday
Monday
Tuesday
Wednesday
Thursday
Friday
Saturday

A. Joe works ___Tuesday___, _____ and _____.
                   1.   2.   3.

B. Sunday, _____, _____ and _____ are his days off.
                4.   5.   6.

98   Answers: 1. Tuesday   2. Thursday   3. Saturday   4. Monday   5. Wednesday   6. Friday

On The Job

Mei works **Monday** (1.) _____ (2.) and _____ (3.).

Sook works _____ (4.) through _____ (5.).

Bertha works Thursday _____ (6.) Monday

Fred works Tuesday through Saturday. He doesn't work on Sunday or Monday. Those are his days off.

Does Fred work on Tuesday? **Yes, he does.** (7.)
Does Fred work on Sunday? **No, he doesn't.** (8.)
Does Fred work on Wednesday? _____ (9.)
Does Fred work on Monday? _____ (10.)

Answers: 1. Monday 2. Wednesday 3. Friday 4. Monday 5. Friday 6. through 7. Yes, he does. 8. No, he doesn't. 9. Yes, he does. 10. No, he doesn't.

99

Lesson 9b

Objectives: talk about work hours / talk about the past

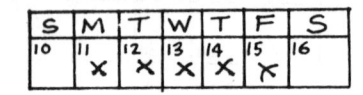

Fred has a new job. He works 9 to 5. He works days.

9 am – 5 pm — days

This week Joe **goes** to work at 4 pm. He **works** the swingshift.

the swingshift

Last week Joe **went** to work at 12 midnight. He **worked** graveyard.

graveyard

He works _days_ .
1.

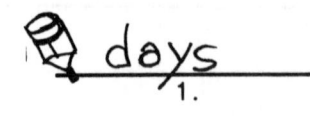

He works the _____ .
2.

He works _____ .
3.

100

Answers: 1. days 2. swingshift 3. graveyard

On The Job

	S	M	T	W	T	F	S
	10	11 X	12 X	13 X	14 X	15 X	16

He works.

He goes to work.

	S	M	T	W	T	F	S
	3	4 X	5 X	6 X	7 X	8 X	9
	10	11	12	13	14	15	16

He worked.

He went to work.

Bob

This week he goes to work at 8 am.
He works days.

Last week he went to work at 4 pm.
He worked the swingshift.

Ron

This week he __goes__ to work at 4 pm.
　　　　　　　1.
He _____ the swingshift.
　　2.

Last week he _____ to work at 12 am.
　　　　　　　　3.
He _____ graveyard.
　　4.

George

This week he _____ to work at 12 am.
　　　　　　　　5.
He _____ graveyard.
　　6.

Last week he _____ to work at 8 am.
　　　　　　　7.
He _____ days.
　　8.

Answers:　1. goes　2. works　3. went　4. worked　5. goes　6. works　7. went　8. worked

Lesson 9c

Objectives: follow directions
talk about locations of items

"Fred works in a warehouse."

"Mr. Smith tells Fred where to stack the boxes."

LEFT ← → RIGHT

A stack   2 stacks

Put it
<u>on</u> <u>top</u> <u>of</u>
the left stack.

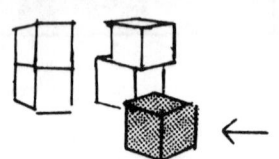

Put it
<u>in</u> <u>front</u> <u>of</u>
the right stack.

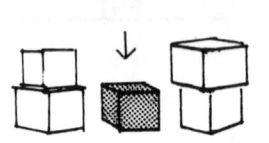

Put it
<u>between</u>
the two stacks.

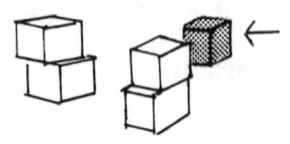

Put it
<u>behind</u>
the right stack.

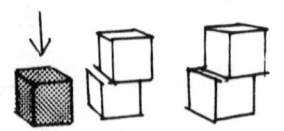

Put it
<u>to</u> <u>the</u> <u>left</u> <u>of</u>
the two stacks.

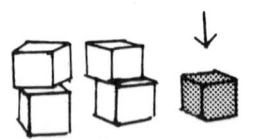

Put it
<u>to</u> <u>the</u> <u>right</u> <u>of</u>
the two stacks.

1. between
2. on top of
3. to the right of
4. to the left of

a.
b.
c.
d.

102

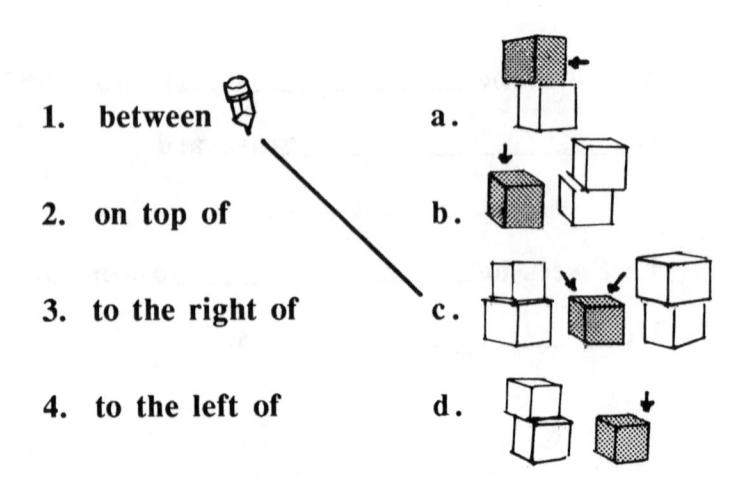

Answers: 1. c 2. a 3. d 4. b

On The Job

Where is the box?

- On top of the right stack.
- In front of the left stack.
- Between the 2 stacks.
- To the right of 2 stacks.
- Behind the left stack.

Where is it?

1. In front of the left stack.
2.
3.
4.
5.
6.

Answers: 1. In front of the left stack.   2. Between the two stacks.   3. To the right of the two stacks.
4. On top of the right stack.   5. To the left of the two stacks.   6. On top of the left stack.

103

Lesson 9d

Objective: ask for help when you don't understand

Mr. Smith: Stack these boxes over there.
Fred: I'm sorry. I don't understand.
Could you explain that again, please?
Mr. Smith: Put these boxes over there.
Fred: Could you speak a little slower, please?
Mr. Smith: Sure. Stack these boxes over there.
Fred: Oh. Okay.

I'm sorry. I don't understand.
Could you explain that again, please?
Could you speak a little slower, please?

On The Job

Mr. Smith: Stack these __boxes__ over there.
                            1.
Fred: I'm _____. I don't _____.
              2.   3.
Could _____ explain _____ again, please?
        4.   5.
Mr. Smith: _____ these boxes over _____.
                6.   7.
Fred: Could you _____ a little _____, please?
                       8.   9.
Mr. Smith: Sure. _____ these boxes _____ there.
                     10.   11.
Fred: Oh. Okay.

Answers: 1. boxes   2. sorry   3. understand   4. you   5. that   6. Put   7. there   8. speak   9. slower
           10. Stack   11. over

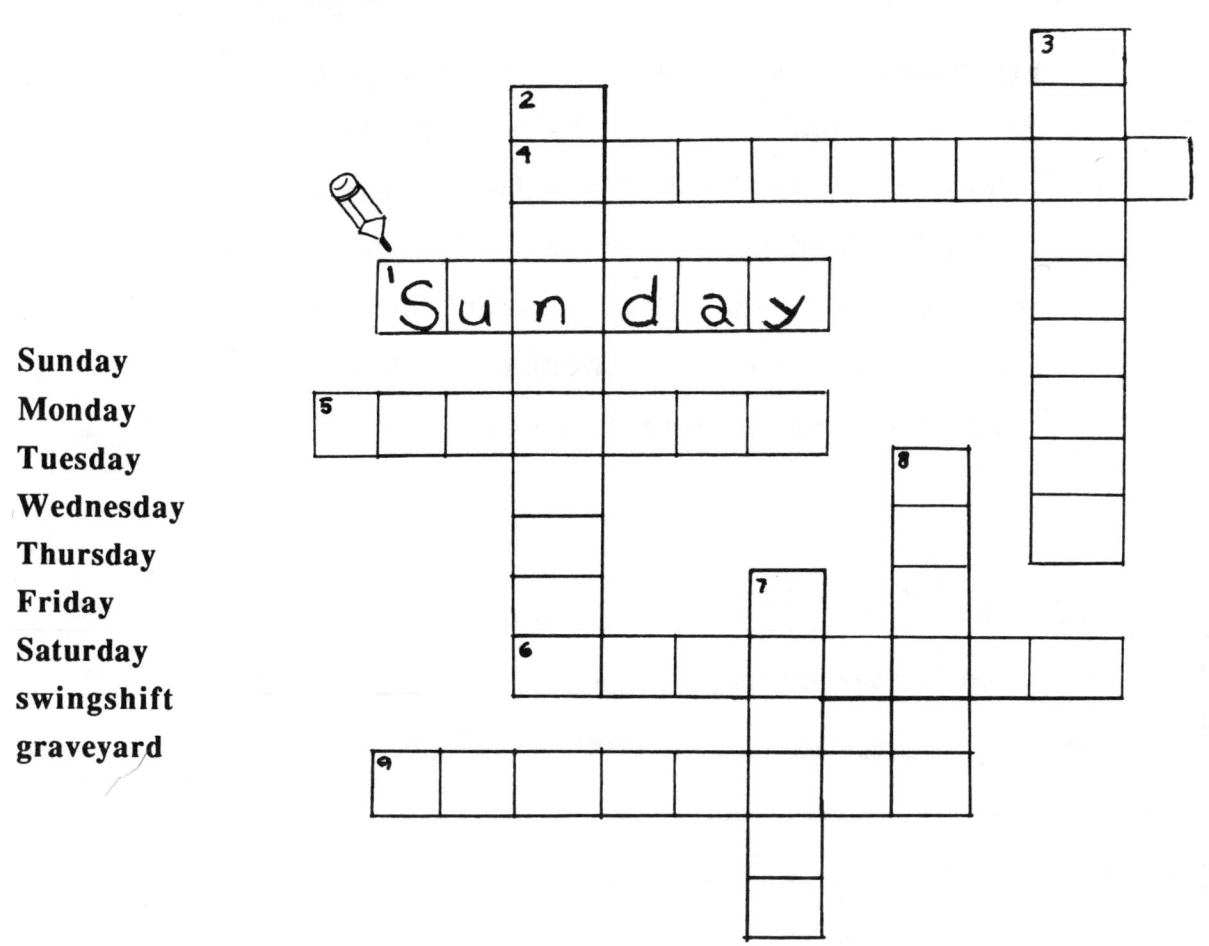

Sunday
Monday
Tuesday
Wednesday
Thursday
Friday
Saturday
swingshift
graveyard

1. Sunday

Answers: 1. Sunday   2. swingshift   3. graveyard   4. Wednesday   5. Tuesday   6. Thursday
           7. Friday   8. Monday   9. Saturday

105

Review 9

Fred has a new job. He works in a warehouse and stacks boxes. This week he has a good schedule. He works Monday through Friday. He works the swingshift. Saturday and Sunday are his days off.

His friend Bob works days. This week he goes to work at 8:00 am. Last week Bob and Fred worked graveyard. They went to work at 12:00 am. They don't like to work graveyard.

A. Fred works ___Monday___ through _____.
                 1.   2.

B. Sunday and Monday are his _____ _____.
                                 3.

C. Fred _____ to work at 4:00 pm.
             4.

D. His friend Bob _____ days.
                       5.

E. Last week they _____ graveyard.
                     6.

Answers: 1. Monday 2. Friday 3. days off 4. goes 5. works 6. worked

On The Job

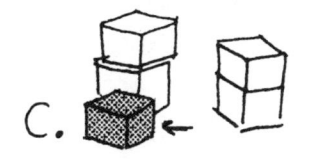

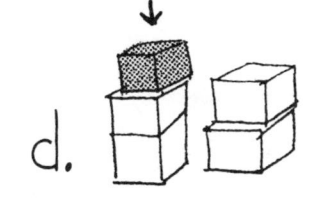

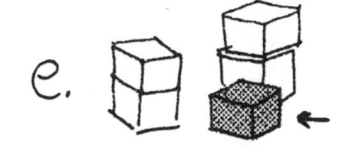

1. between the two stacks
2. to the right of the two stacks
3. behind the right stack
4. in front of the left stack
5. on top of the right stack
6. to the left of the two stacks
7. behind the left stack
8. in front of the right stack
9. on top of the left stack

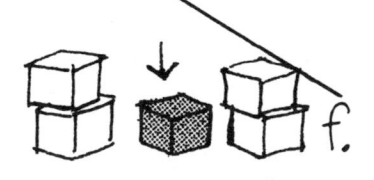

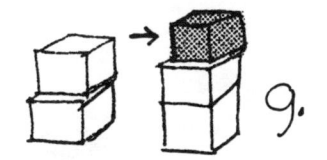

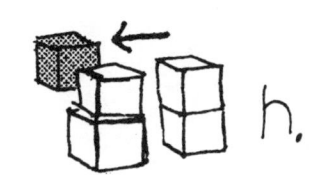

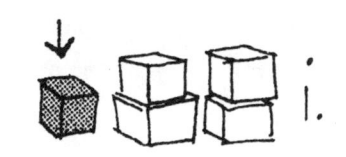

Answers: 1. f 2. b 3. a 4. c 5. g 6. i 7. h 8. e 9. d

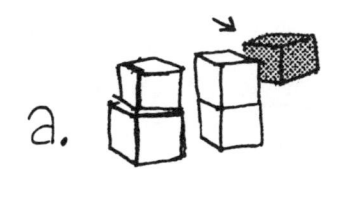

107

Your Notes

Unit 10

Health and Fitness

Lesson 10a

Objective: describe people

Let's talk about height.

SAM — He's tall.
MARIO — He's of average height.
YOKO — She's short.

Let's talk about weight.

FRANK — He's thin.
DEBBIE — She's of average weight.
MIKE — He's heavy.

Who am I describing?

1. He's tall and heavy. — Mike
2. She's short and thin. _____
3. She's of average weight and of average height. _____
4. He's tall and thin. _____
5. He's of average height and of average weight. _____

110

Answers: 1. Mike 2. Yoko 3. Debbie 4. Sam 5. Mario

Health and Fitness

SAM — He has wavy, brown hair.

YOKO — She has straight, black hair.

MIKE — He has curly, red hair.

DEBBIE — She has wavy, blond hair.

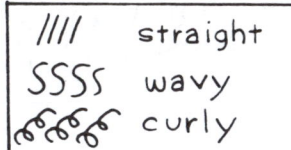

Let's talk about hair.

////	straight
SSSS	wavy
&&&&	curly

Who am I describing?

JOSE   KEN   JIM   NAN   BETTY

1. She's of average height and heavy.
   She has wavy, red hair. — **Nan**

2. He's short and heavy.
   He has straight, black hair. _____

3. He's tall and of average weight.
   He has curly, black hair. _____

4. She's short and thin.
   She has straight, blond hair. _____

5. He's of average height and weight.
   He has straight, brown hair. _____

Answers: 1. Nan 2. Jose 3. Jim 4. Betty 5. Ken

111

Lesson 10b

Objective: talk about getting a medical check-up

Tom gets a medical check-up once a year.

The doctor asks Tom some questions.

I smoke a lot.

How much do you smoke?

Tom smokes a lot.

Tom drinks a lot.

Tom excercises a little.

He smokes a lot.

How much does Tom smoke?

How much does Tom drink?   _He drinks a lot._
                                1.

How much does Tom exercise? _____
                                2.

Tom should take better care of himself.

should = good for you

He _should smoke_ less.
      3.

He _____ less.
      4.

He _____ more.
      5.

Answers: 1. He drinks a lot. 2. He exercises a little. 3. should smoke 4. should drink 5. should exercise

112

Health and Fitness

LESS (−)	MORE (+)
sugar salt	vegetables fruit
red meat butter and oil	fish poultry

The doctor put Tom on a diet.

Tom should eat   **more   vegetables**.
1.

Tom should eat _____ _____.
2.

Tom should eat _____ _____.
3.

Tom should eat _____ _____.
4.

Tom should eat _____ _____.
5.

Tom should eat _____ _____.
6.

Tom went to the doctor for a check-up. The doctor said he should smoke and drink less. He also said Tom should exercise more and should go on a diet. He should eat more fruit and vegetables and less sugar, salt, butter and oil.

Answers: 1. more vegetables 2. less salt 3. less butter 4. more fish
5. less red meat 6. more fruit

113

Lesson 10c

Objective: talk about exercising

"Tom followed the doctor's directions."
"Now he eats less and exercises more."

TOM
He rides a bike.
He swims.
He walks.

"What does Frank do?"

FRANK

"He jogs."

What does Sam do?
He _plays_ basketball.
1.

What does Mario do?
He _____ soccer.
2.

What does Debbie do?
She _____ tennis.
3.

I swim.	He swims.
I walk.	He walks.
I play soccer.	He plays soccer.
I ride a bicycle.	He rides a bicycle.

Answers: 1. plays 2. plays 3. plays

Health and Fitness

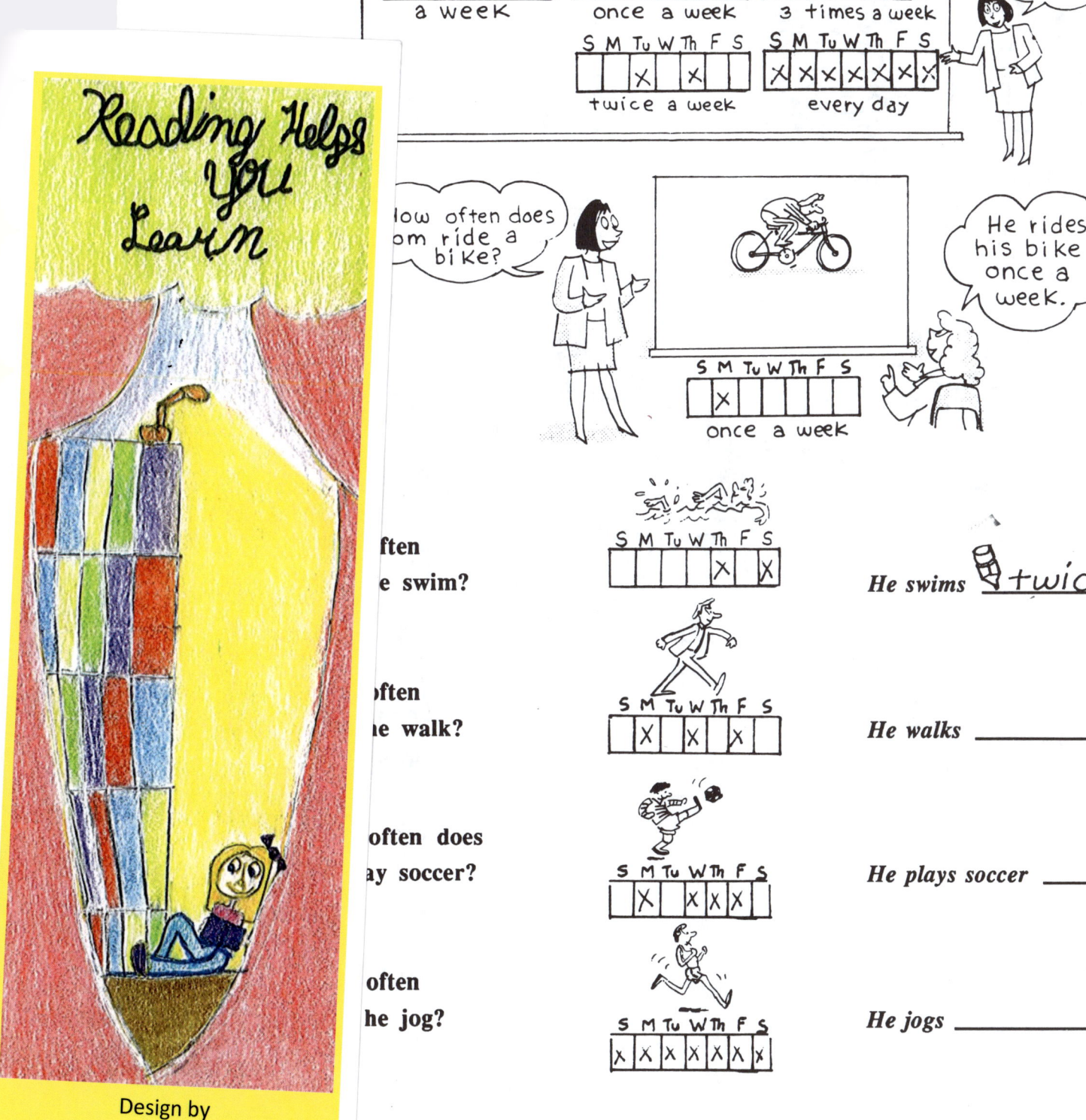

"Let's talk about how often people exercise."

S M Tu W Th F S	S M Tu W Th F S	S M Tu W Th F S
a week	once a week	3 times a week

S M Tu W Th F S	S M Tu W Th F S
twice a week	every day

"How often does Tom ride a bike?" "He rides his bike once a week."

S M Tu W Th F S — once a week

How often does he swim? — He swims <u>twice a week</u>. 1.

How often does he walk? — He walks _____. 2.

How often does he play soccer? — He plays soccer _____. 3.

How often does he jog? — He jogs _____. 4.

Answers: 1. twice a week 2. 3 times a week 3. 4 times a week 4. every day

115

Reading Helps You Learn

Design by **Hannah Waddell**
Age 9

Lesson 10d

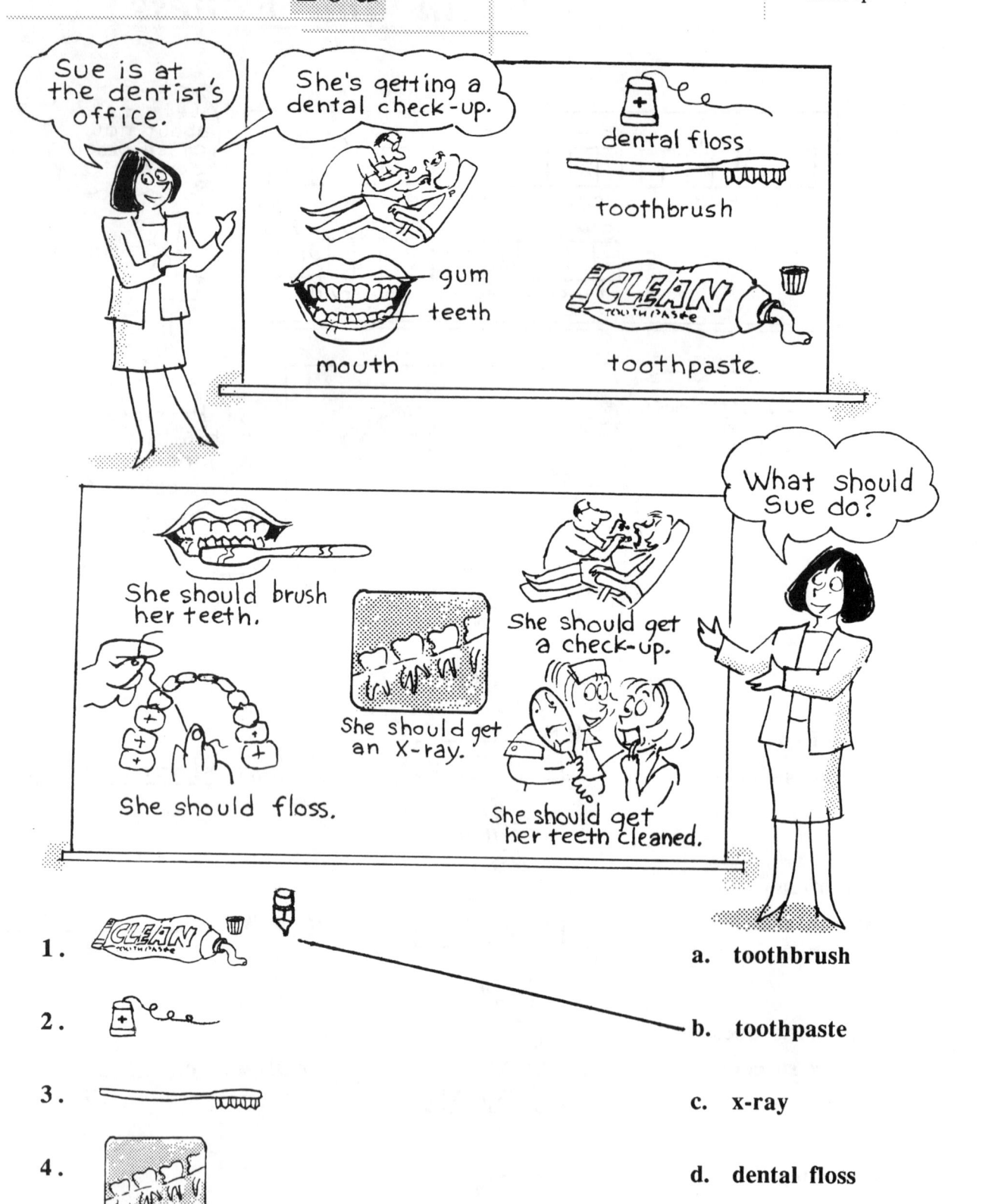

Objective talk about getting a dental check-up

"Sue is at the dentist's office."

"She's getting a dental check-up."

- dental floss
- toothbrush
- gum
- teeth
- mouth
- toothpaste

"What should Sue do?"

- She should brush her teeth.
- She should floss.
- She should get an X-ray.
- She should get a check-up.
- She should get her teeth cleaned.

1. a. toothbrush
2. b. toothpaste
3. c. x-ray
4. d. dental floss

116

Answers: 1. b 2. d 3. a 4. c

Health and Fitness

How often should she brush her teeth?

How often should she floss?  — Once a day. 1.

How often should she brush her teeth? _____ 2.

How often should she get an x-ray? _____ 3.

How often should she get her teeth cleaned? _____ 4.

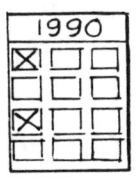

Answers: 1. Once a day. 2. Twice a day. 3. Once a year. 4. Twice a year.

117

Review 10

Tom wants to take care of himself. He goes to a doctor for a medical check-up once a year. He drinks a little, but he doesn't smoke. He also goes to a dentist twice a year. The dentist checks Tom's teeth after he gets his teeth cleaned.

Tom exercises a little. He plays soccer on Saturdays. He should exercise more.

1. Tom goes for a medical check-up once a year. (Yes) No

2. Tom smokes a lot. Yes No

3. Tom never drinks. Yes No

4. The dentist checks Tom's teeth. Yes No

5. Tom plays soccer every day. Yes No

Answers: 1. Yes 2. No 3. No 4. Yes 5. No

118

Health and Fitness

1. vegetables 2. fish 3. red meat 4. salt 5. oil 6. poultry 7. butter 8. fruit

What do they do? How often?

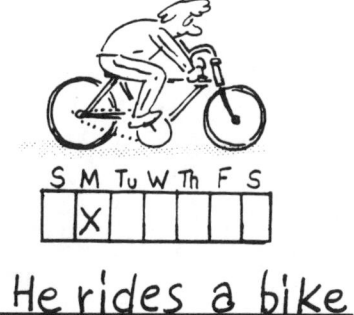

He rides a bike once a week.

9.

10. _____

11. _____

12. _____

Answers: 1. b 2. c 3. d 4. a 5. f 6. h 7. e 8. g 9. He rides a bike once a week.
10. He walks twice a week. 11. She plays soccer 3 times a week. 12. She swims twice a week.

119

Your Notes

Unit 11

Buying a Car

Lesson 11a

Objectives: express preferences
describe types of cars

"Joe takes the bus to work, but he wants to buy a car."

"He can buy a used car or a new car."

"A compact car."

"What is it?"

sedan
What is it?
A sedan.
1.

van
What is it?
2.

station wagon
What is it?
3.

sports car
What is it?
4.

122   Answers: 1. A sedan.   2. A van.   3. A station wagon.   4. A sports car.

Buying a Car

The Sanchez family wants to buy a used car.

Joe: We're looking for a used car.
Salesman: This compact is a good-looking car.
Joe: It's too small. We want a bigger car.
Salesman: The sedan is bigger than the compact.
Joe: It's O.K. But we want a roomier car.
Salesman: This is a nice, roomy car.
Joe: It's perfect. We want a van.

Which car is **more** expensive?

$9,000 — expensive
$12,000 — more expensive

The station wagon is _expensive_.
                          1.
The van is _____ _____
                              2.
than the station wagon.

Answers: 1. expensive 2. more expensive

123

Lesson 11b

Objective compare different types of cars

We compare cars before we buy them.

roomy

A station wagon is **roomier than** a sedan.

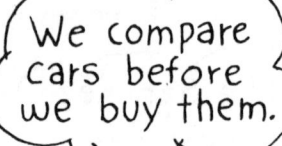

big

A van is **bigger than** a station wagon.

fast

A sports car is **faster than** a compact.

small

A sports car is **smaller than** a compact.

A ___van___ is bigger than a _____.
     1.   2.

A _____ is faster than a _____.
     3.   4.

124

Answers: 1. van   2. compact   3. sports car   4. compact

Buying a Car

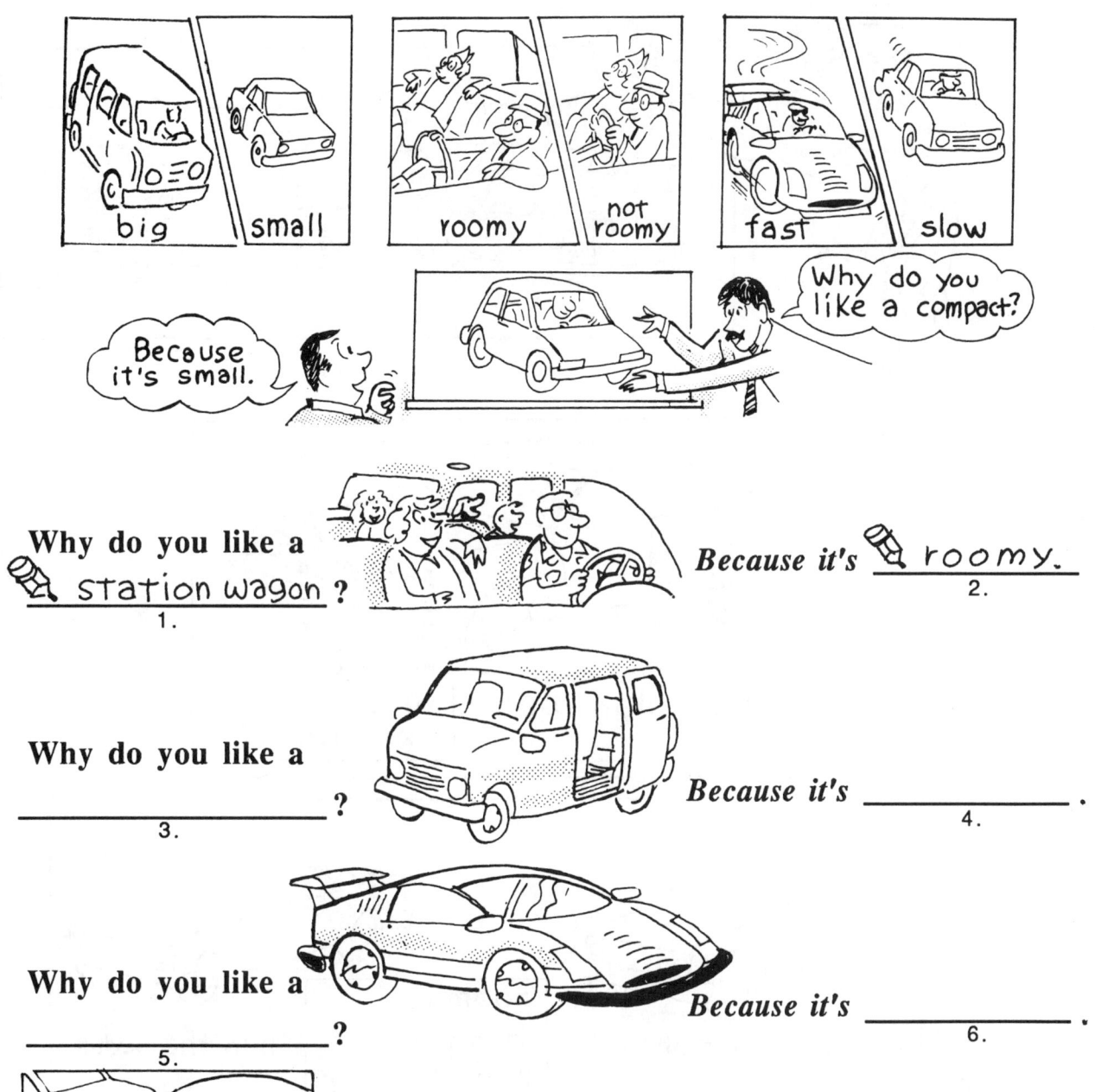

big | small   roomy | not roomy   fast | slow

"Why do you like a compact?"

"Because it's small."

Why do you like a <u>station wagon</u>?
1.

Because it's <u>roomy</u>.
2.

Why do you like a _____?
3.

Because it's _____.
4.

Why do you like a _____?
5.

Because it's _____.
6.

Joe wants to buy a car. He can buy a used car or a new car. He can look on the street for one, or he can go to a dealer. There are many types of cars he can buy.

Answers: 1. station wagon 2. roomy 3. van 4. big 5. sports car 6. fast

Lesson 11c

Objectives compare different types of cars
talk about the past

The Sanchez family looked at many cars.

The sedan was | roomy.
| big.
| expensive.

The station wagon was | roomier
| bigger | than the sedan.
| more expensive

The van was | the roomiest
| the biggest | car.
| the most expensive

126

Buying a Car

Listen to Joe and his friend.

Joe: I bought a car last week.
Friend: What type of car did you buy?
Joe: I bought a van.
Friend: Why did you buy a van?
Joe: I needed the roomiest car for my family.
Friend: Where did you get it?
Joe: I got it at Bob's Auto Sales.
Friend: Did you drive it to work today?
Joe: No, my wife drove me.

1. Joe bought a station wagon. Yes **No**
2. He needed a fast car. Yes No
3. He got it at Bob's Auto Sales. Yes No
4. He drove it to work. Yes No

What type of car <u>did</u> you <u>buy</u>? I <u>bought</u> a van.
Where <u>did</u> you <u>get</u> it? I <u>got</u> it at Bob's Auto Sales.
<u>Did</u> you <u>drive</u> it to work today? No, my wife <u>drove</u> me.

Answers: 1. No 2. No 3. Yes 4. No

127

Lesson 11d

Objectives learn about car maintenance
learn to request car maintenance

battery

gasoline (gas)

tires

oil

radiator

Mr. and Mrs. Sanchez went to the gas station yesterday. She bought the most expensive gas. She also checked her tires. Her husband checked the battery and the radiator. She put air in the tires. Her husband put water in the battery and in the radiator.

1. Mrs. Sanchez bought the cheapest gas.   Yes   *No*
2. Her husband put water in the radiator.   Yes   No
3. Mrs. Sanchez put water in the tires.   Yes   No
4. Her husband put air in the battery.   Yes   No

128

Answers: 1. No   2. Yes   3. No   4. No

Buying a Car

If the car has problems, ask for help.

Mrs. Sanchez: Could you check the tires and the battery?
Mr. Sanchez: Sure . . . the battery needs water, and the tires need air.

Mrs. Sanchez: The engine is running hot. Could you check the radiator?
Mr. Sanchez: All right . . . the water is low.

Mrs. Sanchez: The car doesn't start. Could you check the battery?
Mr. Sanchez: All right . . . the battery is dead.

What does this part of the car need?

1. A tire needs ___air___.
2. A battery needs _____.
3. A radiator needs _____.
4. An engine needs _____.

Answers: 1. air   2. water   3. water   4. oil

Review 11

Last week Joe bought a used van for his family at Bob's Auto Sales. The van is roomy but not very fast. The fastest car that he saw was a sports car. It was faster than the van, and it was more expensive. The van was cheaper than the sports car, but it was not the cheapest car that he saw. The cheapest car was the compact. Joe and his family are very happy in their van. Joe drives to work, and on Saturday and Sunday Joe and his family go many places.

1. Joe bought a station wagon last week.   Yes   *No*
2. Joe bought the car at Bob's Auto Sales.   Yes   No
3. Joe wanted a small car.   Yes   No
4. The van was faster than the sports car.   Yes   No
5. The van was more expensive than the sports car.   Yes   No
6. Joe drives the van to work.   Yes   No

130   Answers: 1. No 2. Yes 3. No 4. No 5. No 6. Yes

Buying a Car

What is it?

A van.
1.

2.

3.

4.

What can you do?

5. The car doesn't start.   a. Put air in them.
6. The engine is running hot.   b. Check the battery.
7. The tires need air.   c. Put oil in it.
8. The car has no gas.   d. Check the radiator.
9. The car has no oil.   e. Put gas in the car.

Answers: 1. A van.   2. A sports car.   3. A station wagon.   4. A sedan.
5. b   6. d   7. a   8. e   9. c

131

Your Notes

Unit 12

Apartment Living

Lesson 12a

Objectives: identify furniture
talk about moving to a new apartment

The Johnson family is moving to a new apartment.

They have lots of furniture.

lamp, end table, plant, sofa, television, coffee table, armchair, bookcase

Is this a plant?		Yes, it is.
Is this a television?		No, it isn't.
Is this an end table?		_____
Is this an armchair?		_____
Is this a bookcase?		_____
Is this a coffee table?		_____

Answers: 1. Yes, it is. 2. No, it isn't. 3. Yes, it is. 4. Yes, it is. 5. Yes, it is.
6. No, it isn't.

134

Apartment Living

"Next to the sofa."

"Where does the end table go?"

"Tom is telling his friends where to put the furniture."

Where does the sofa go?

Between ~~the windows~~.
1.

Where does the bookcase go?

Against _____ _____.
2.

Where does the coffee table go?

In front of _____ _____.
3.

Where does the lamp go?

On _____ _____.
4.

Where does the plant go?

Behind _____ _____.
5.

6. Where is the armchair?
7. Where is the television?
8. Where is the bookcase?
9. Where is the coffee table?
10. Where is the plant?

a. Against the wall.
b. Behind the sofa.
c. On the coffee table.
d. In front of the sofa.
e. Between the windows.

Answers: 1. the windows   2. the wall   3. the sofa   4. the end table   5. the armchair
6. e   7. c   8. a   9. d   10. b

135

Lesson **12b** Objective | report a problem

"There are some problems in the new apartment."

The heater isn't working.

The oven isn't working.

The light switch isn't working.

The refrigerator isn't working.

The outlet isn't working.

The shower isn't working.

"The oven isn't working."

"What's the problem?"

1. The refrigerator isn't working.
2. _____
3. _____
4. _____
5. _____

Answers: 1. The refrigerator isn't working. 2. The light switch isn't working. 3. The shower isn't working. 4. The outlet isn't working. 5. The heater isn't working.

136

Apartment Living

Sue is calling the manager. She needs a plumber.

Sue: This is Sue Johnson in Apartment 3C.
The heater isn't working.

Manager: Oh. Sorry about that.
I'll call the plumber.

Sue: **This** _____ Sue Johnson in Apartment 3C.
   1.   2.
The _____ isn't _____.
        3.   4.

Manager: Oh. _____ about that.
                 5.
I'll _____ the _____.
        6.   7.

A_____ fixes ovens and refrigerators.
   8.

A_____ fixes showers and heaters.
   9.

An_____ fixes outlets and light switches.
    10.

Answers: 1. This 2. is 3. heater 4. working 5. Sorry 6. call 7. plumber 8. repairman
9. plumber 10. electrician

137

Lesson 12c

Objectives
talk about ho...
talk about the future

"The Johnson family is talking about housework."

Bill is going to mop the floor.

Mary is going to wash the dishes.

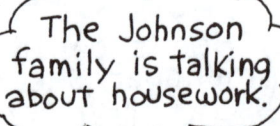

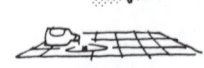

Tom is going to take out the trash.

Sue is going to do the laundry.

Tom is going to vacuum the carpet.

Mary is going to make the beds.

1. do the laundry
2. take out the trash
3. wash the dishes
4. vacuum the carpet
5. mop the floor
6. make the beds

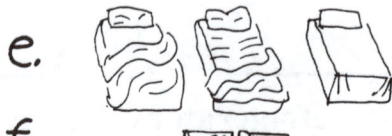

a.
b.
c.
d.
e.
f.

Answers: 1. f 2. a 3. c 4. d 5. b 6. e

138

Apartment Living

What is Tom going to do?

1. Tom is going to take out the trash.

What is Bill going to do?

2. _____

What is Sue going to do?

3. _____

Tom **is**
Bill and Mary **are** going to make the beds.

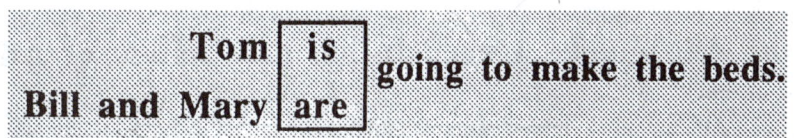

What are Bill and Mary going to do?

4. Bill and Mary are going to do the laundry.

What are Tom and Sue going to do?

5. _____
_____

What are Tom and Mary going to do?

6. _____
_____

Answers: 1. Tom is going to take out the trash. 2. Bill is going to mop the floor. 3. Sue is going to do the laundry. 4. Bill and Mary are going to do the laundry. 5. Tom and Sue are going to wash the dishes. 6. Tom and Mary are going to mop the floor.

Lesson 12d

Objectives introduce yourself to your neighbors
fill out a "Change of Address" form

Sue Johnson is meeting her new neighbor.

Hi. I'm Minh Lee.
Hi. I'm Sue Johnson.

Sue Johnson: Hi. I'm Sue Johnson. I just moved into Apartment 3C.

Minh Lee: Hi. I'm Minh Lee. I live in Apartment 2E.

Sue Johnson: Maybe you can help me. Is there a post office near here?

Minh Lee: Yes. There's one on 5th Street.

Sue Johnson: Oh, good. I need to get a "Change of Address" form.

Is there a park near here?
Yes, there's one on 5th Street.

1. Is there <u>a market</u> <u>near here?</u> ?
   Yes, <u>there's one</u> <u>on 5th Street</u>.

2. Is there _____
   _____?
   Yes, _____
   _____.

3. Is there _____
   _____?
   Yes, _____
   _____.

Answers: 1. Is there a market near here?
Yes, there's one on 5th Street.

2. Is there a bank near here?
Yes, there's one on 1st. Avenue.

3. Is there a bakery near here?
Yes, there's one on 5th Street.

Apartment Living

Old Apartment

946 Montana St. #6
Los Angeles, CA 90012

New Apartment

1323 S. Elm Ave. Apt. 3C
Van Nuys, CA 91411

When you move, you fill out a "Change of Address" form from the post office.

Fill out a form for the Johnson family.

CHANGE OF ADDRESS FORM

OLD ADDRESS
Print or type last name
① Johnson, Sue, Tom, Mary and Bill
② Street no. — apt.
③ city — state — zip

NEW ADDRESS
④ street no. — apt.
⑤ city — state — zip

Effective date: May 1
Date signed: May 3
Signature: *Sue Johnson*

Change of address is for
☒ family
☐ individual

effective date = the date you move

Answers: 1. Johnson, Sue, Tom, Mary and Bill 2. 946 Montana St. #6 3. Los Angeles, CA 90012 4. 1323 S. Elm Ave. Apt. 3C 5. Van Nuys, CA 91411

Review 12

Sue Johnson and her family live in a new apartment. There are some problems. The heater isn't working, and the shower isn't working. She has to call the manager for a plumber. She also has to go to the post office for a "Change of Address" form. There is a post office on 5th Street near her apartment.

The Johnson family also has a lot of work to do in the apartment. Today after breakfast, Sue is going to wash the dishes. Tom, her husband, is going to vacuum the carpet. Bill and Mary, the children, are going to make the beds and take out the trash. The apartment is going to be very clean!

1.	The Johnson family live in a new apartment.	(Yes)	No
2.	The shower isn't working.	Yes	No
3.	The post office is on 2nd Street.	Yes	No
4.	After breakfast, Sue is going to vacuum.	Yes	No
5.	Bill and Mary are going to mop the floor.	Yes	No

Answers: 1. Yes   2. Yes   3. No   4. No   5. No

Apartment Living

a.

b.

c.

d.

1. plant
2. television
3. end table
4. armchair
5. bookcase
6. coffee table
7. sofa
8. lamp

e.

f.

g.

h.

9. Where is the plant? ✎ Between the windows.
10. Where is the coffee table? _____
11. Where is the bookcase? _____
12. Where is the television? _____
13. Where is the lamp? _____

Answers: 1. b 2. c 3. e 4. h 5. a 6. d 7. g 8. f 9. Between the windows.
10. In front of the sofa. 11. Against the wall. 12. On the coffee table.
13. On the end table.

143

Your Notes

Unit 13

Special Occasions

Lesson 13a

Objectives: talk about feelings / talk about frequency

1. Fred __is homesick__.

2. Joe _____ _____.

3. Fred _____ _____.

4. Joe _____ _____.

5. Joe and Fred _____ _____.

146   Answers: 1. is homesick   2. is bored   3. is sad   4. isn't homesick   5. are happy

Special Occasions

Is Fred homesick?
Yes, he is.

Is Joe homesick?  — Is Fred sad?  — Is Fred happy?  — Is Joe bored?

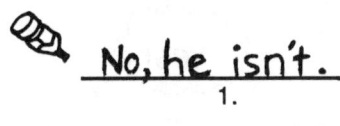

1. <u>No, he isn't.</u>   2. _____   3. _____   4. _____

Are you **ever** bored?
No, I'm **never** bored.

Are you **ever** sad?
Yes, I'm **sometimes** sad.

Are you **ever** homesick?
Yes, I'm **always** homesick.

always	100%
sometimes	50%
never	0%

Answers: 1. No, he isn't.   2. No, he isn't.   3. No, he isn't.   4. Yes, he is.

147

Lesson 13b

Objectives: extend an invitation / refuse an invitation / accept an invitation

Fred: We are having a party for Bill on Saturday. Would you like to come?

Joe: (Yes) _____
1.

Sam: (No) _____
2.

Answers: 1. Sounds great! I'd love to. 2. I'm sorry, but I already have plans.

Special Occasions

"We are going to a baseball game on Saturday. Would you like to come?"

"Sounds great! I'd love to."

"I'm sorry, but I already have plans."

the zoo / Sunday

1. We are going to the zoo on Sunday. Would you like to come?

the beach / Saturday

2. _____

Disneyland / Friday

3. _____

a concert / Tuesday

4. _____

Answers:
1. We are going to the zoo on Sunday. Would you like to come?
2. We are going to the beach on Saturday. Would you like to come?
3. We are going to Disneyland on Friday. Would you like to come?
4. We are going to a concert on Tuesday. Would you like to come?

Lesson 13c

Objectives
talk about birthday parties
talk about feelings
ask someone out on a date

"Fred needs to buy a birthday present and a birthday card for the party."

birthday cake
1.

birthday _____
2.

birthday _____
3.

"How does Fred feel about the party?"

excited   nervous

Fred is _____ about the party.
4.

Fred is _____ about the party.
5.

150   Answers: 1. cake   2. present   3. card   4. nervous   5. excited

Special Occasions

Mary: Hi. I'm Mary White.
Fred: Hi. I'm Fred Jones. Nice to meet you.
Mary: Nice to meet you, too.

(Later...)

Fred: Would you like to go to a concert on Saturday?
Mary: Sounds great! I'd love to.

Mary: Hi. I'm __Mary__ __White__.
                    1.
Fred: Hi. I'm Fred Jones. Nice to _____ you.
                                       2.
Mary: _____ to meet you, too.
           3.

(Later...)

Fred: _____ you like to go to a _____
          4.   5.
on Saturday?

Mary: Sounds _____ ! I'd love to.
                  6.

Answers: 1. Mary White   2. meet   3. Nice   4. Would   5. concert   6. great

151

Lesson 13d

Objective: talk about frequency

*Fred is **sometimes** nervous at parties. Are you nervous at parties?*

*Yes, I'm **always** nervous at parties.*

always	.... 100%
(all of the time)	
usually	....
(most of the time)	
sometimes	.... 50%
(some of the time)	
seldom	....
(almost never)	
never	.... 0%
(not at any time)	

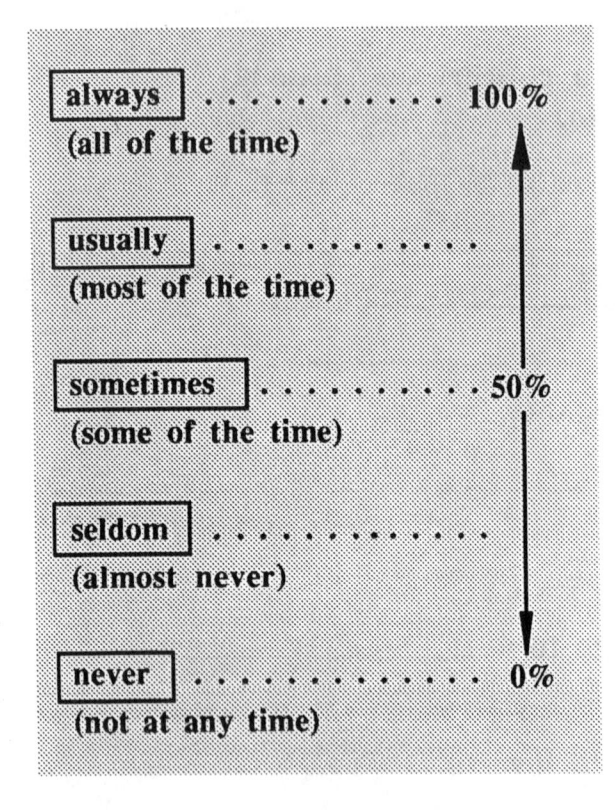

1. always   a. most of the time

2. usually   b. not at any time

3. sometimes   c. all of the time

4. seldom   d. some of the time

5. never   e. almost never

Answers: 1. c   2. a   3. d   4. e   5. b

Special Occasions

1. Fred is nervous around women <u>all of the time</u>.
   Fred is <u>always</u> nervous around women.

2. Fred and Joe are bored <u>some of the time</u>.
   Fred and Joe are _____ bored.

3. Joe is <u>not</u> homesick <u>at any time</u>.
   Joe is _____ homesick.

4. Rover is happy <u>most of the time</u>.
   Rover is _____ happy.

Answers: 1. always   2. sometimes   3. never   4. usually

153

Review 13

We are having a party for Bill on Saturday. Would you like to come?

Fred and Joe are going to have a party for Bill on Saturday. They invite many friends to the party.

Fred needs to buy a birthday present and a birthday card for Bill. Fred is excited! He is also a little nervous about meeting women at the party. He is usually nervous around women.

1. Fred and Joe are going to have a party.   Yes   No
2. They invite many friends.   Yes   No
3. Fred needs to buy a birthday card.   Yes   No
4. Fred is sad about the party.   Yes   No
5. He is always nervous around women.   Yes   No

Answers: 1. Yes 2. Yes 3. Yes 4. No 5. No

Special Occasions

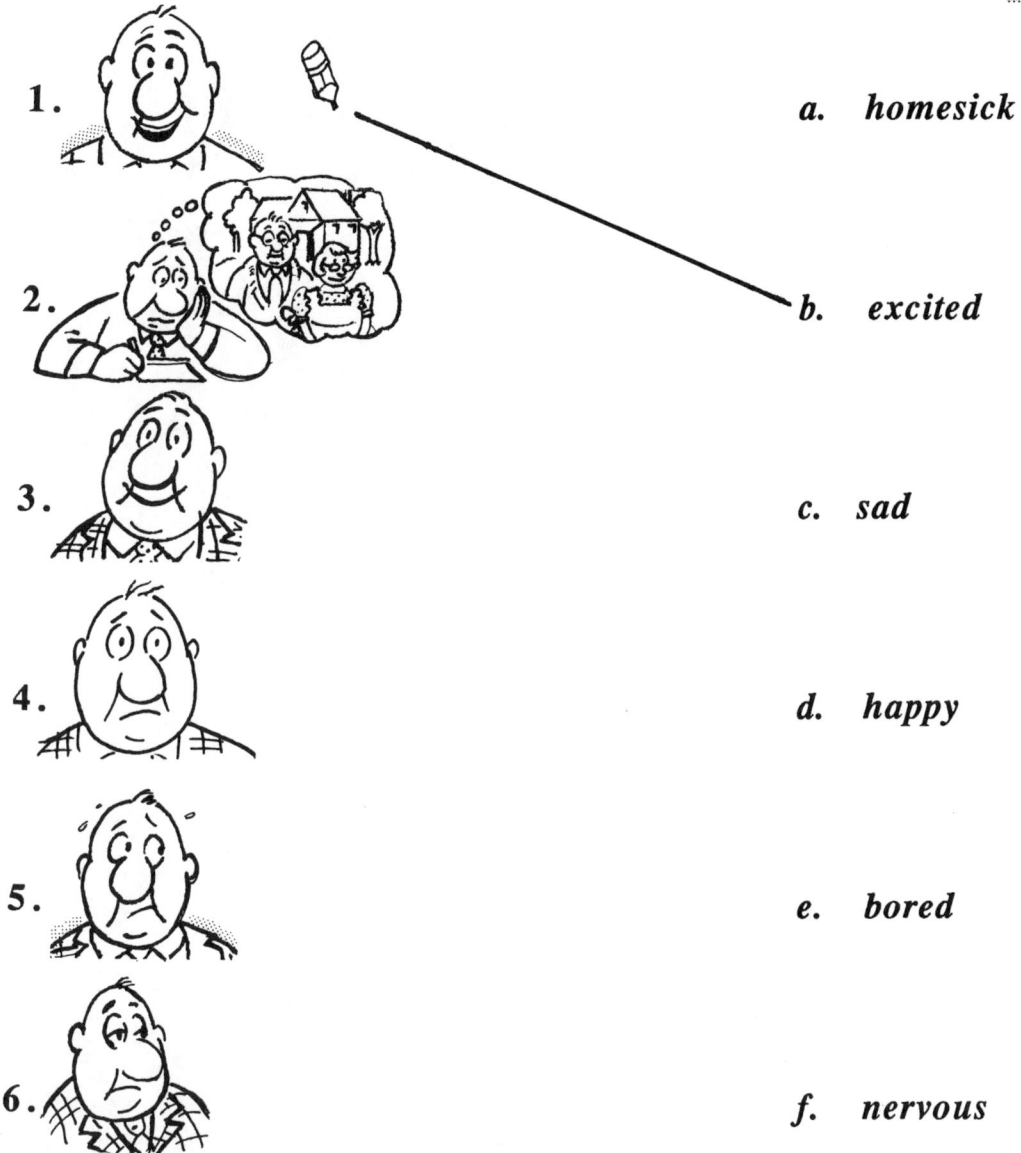

1.
2.
3.
4.
5.
6.

a. homesick
b. excited
c. sad
d. happy
e. bored
f. nervous

---

excited   great   concert   like

Fred: We are going to a _____ on Saturday.
7.
Would you _____ to come?
8.
Mary: Sounds _____ ! I'd love to.
9.
Fred: Good. I'm _____ about the concert.
10.
I'm happy you're coming. See you then.

Answers: 1. b   2. a   3. d   4. c   5. f   6. e   7. concert   8. like   9. great   10. excited

155

Your Notes

Unit 14

Getting Around The City

Lesson 14a

Objectives: ask for directions
give directions

This is Charly Sanchez. He's going to Jim's house but he can't find it.

Charly is lost. He calls Jim on the telephone.

Hi, Jim. This is Charly.
I'm looking for your house, but I'm lost.

Where are you?

I'm at Bob's market.

No problem. Go straight ahead 2 blocks, then turn left on Gail Ave. My house is on the next corner.

Getting Around the City

I'm __at__ Bob's Market. I'm _____ for
    1.   2.
the Post Office.

Walk _____ ahead 1 _____ and
           3.   4.
cross Maple Ave.

I'm _____ Bob's Market. I'm _____ for
      5.   6.
the gas station.

Go 1 block, then turn left on Maple Ave. Go 1
_____ , then _____ right on Main St.
       7.   8.

Answers: 1. at 2. looking 3. straight 4. block 5. at 6. looking 7. block 8. turn

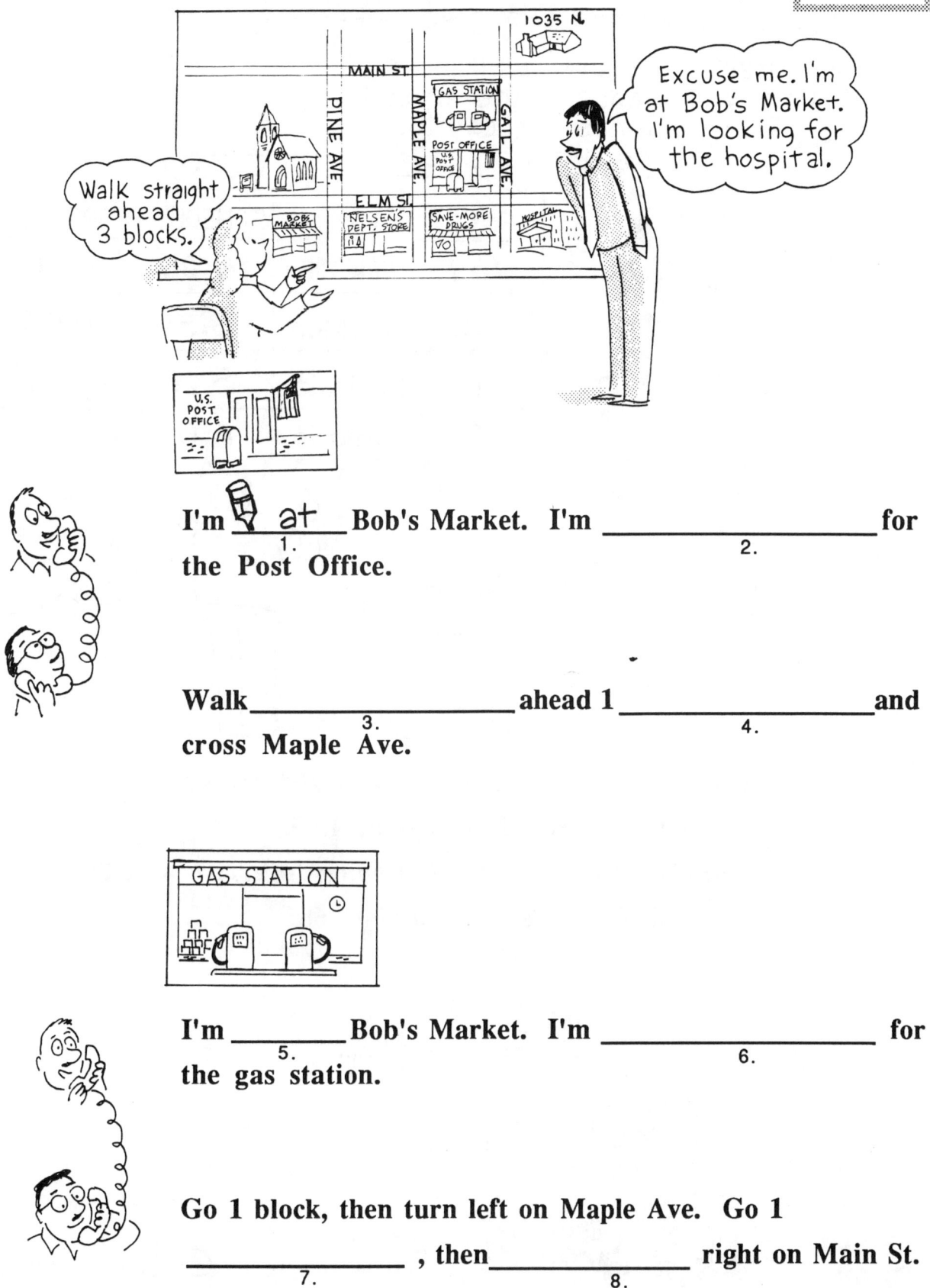

159

Lesson 14b

Objective — read airline schedules

Charly and Jim want to pick up their friends at the airport. Their friends are coming by airplane.

ARRIVALS				
FLIGHT	FROM	SCHEDULED	ARRIVAL	GATE
164	NEW YORK	4:00	4:20	68
320	Chicago	3:54	4:05	75
102	Detroit	5:20	on time	60
730	Ontario	6:00	on time	12

What time does flight 164 arrive?

The schedule says at 4:00.

Charly: What time does Flight 164 arrive?

Jim: The schedule says at 4:00.

Charly: But it's late. It's going to arrive at 4:20.

Jim: OK. Let's go to Gate 68.

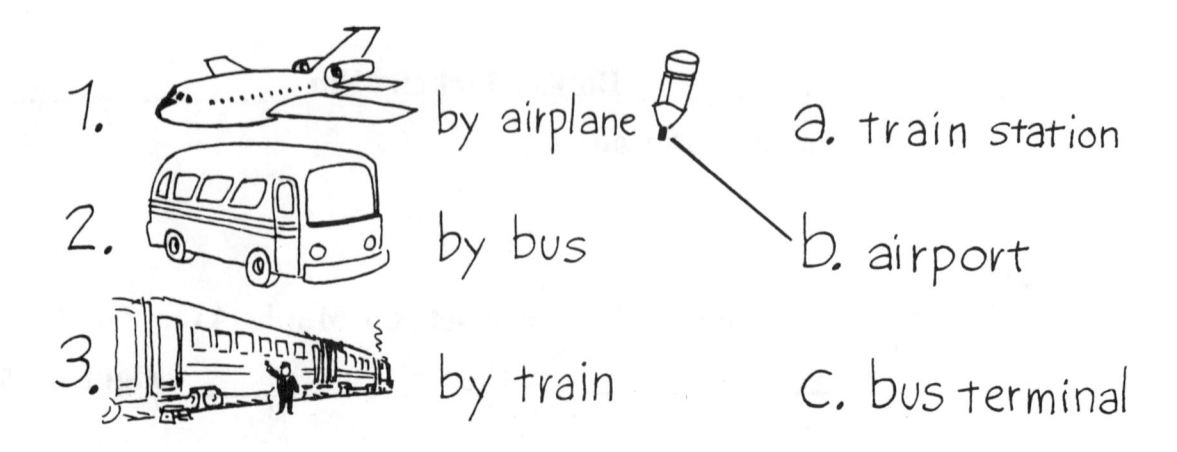

1. by airplane — a. train station
2. by bus — b. airport
3. by train — c. bus terminal

160

Answers: 1. b 2. c 3. a

Getting Around the City

Where does Flight 783 come from?

ARRIVALS

FLIGHT	FROM	SCHEDULED	ARRIVAL	GATE
163	Phoenix	1:30	1:45	63
783	Honolulu	10:00	on time	53
	Chicago	7:28	on time	42
210	Denver	10:00	10:08	21

It comes from Honolulu.

Where does Flight 783 come from?   It comes from Honolulu.

What time does it arrive?   It arrives at 10:00. It's on time.

At what gate does it arrive?   It arrives at Gate 53.

ARRIVALS

FLIGHT	FROM	SCHEDULED	ARRIVAL	GATE
374	Phoenix	6:15	on time	34
110	New York	7:10	on time	10
801	Miami	8:25	8:30	22

Where does Flight 374 come from?   It comes from _____ .
                                                    1.
What time does it arrive?   It arrives at _____ .
                                            2.
At what gate does it arrive?   It arrives at _____ .
                                                3.

Answers: 1. Phoenix   2. 6:15   3. Gate 34

161

Lesson 14c

Objectives: give directions / follow directions

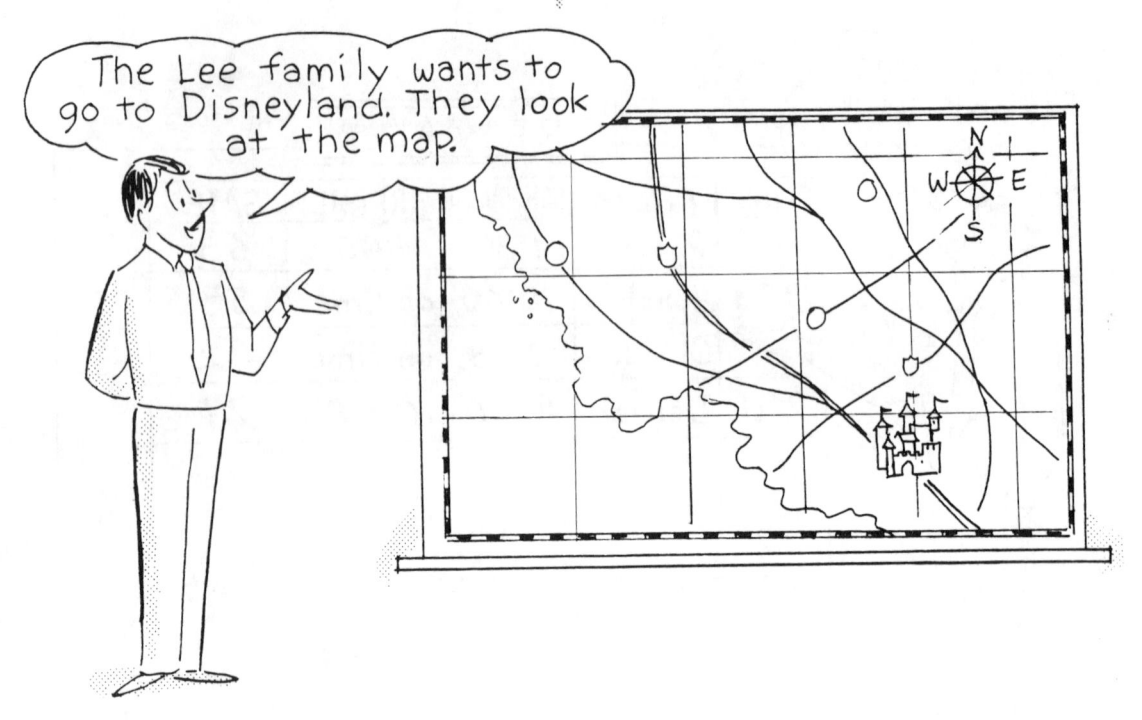

The Lee family wants to go to Disneyland. They look at the map.

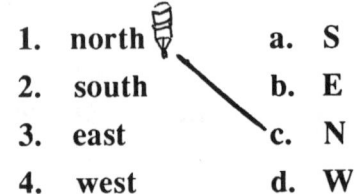

1. north   a. S
2. south   b. E
3. east   c. N
4. west   d. W

How far is it to Disneyland?
How long does it take by car?
It's about 25 miles.
It takes about an hour.

Get on Highway 5 at Pine Ave. Go south.
Then exit at Harbor Blvd.

162   Answers: 1. c   2. a   3. b   4. d

Getting Around the City

How far is it to the zoo?

It's about 10 miles.

How long does it take by car?

It takes about 20 minutes.

**Get on Highway 134 at Willow St. Go east.
Then exit at Victory Blvd.**

1. It's about 10 miles to the zoo.   Yes   No
2. It takes about an hour by car.   Yes   No
3. Get on the highway at Pine Ave.   Yes   No
4. Go west on Highway 134.   Yes   No
5. Exit at Willow St.   Yes   No

Answers: 1. Yes 2. No 3. No 4. No 5. No

163

Lesson 14d

Objective: learn how to take the bus

"The Lee family takes the bus to the beach."

1. They wait for the bus.
2. They get on the bus. 
3. They pay the fare. 
4. They ask for a transfer. 
5. They change to another bus. 
6. They get off the bus at the beach. 

164

Getting Around the City

1. They wait for the bus. 2. _____ 3. _____

4. _____ 5. _____ 6. _____

"The Lee family is going home to New York."

The Lee family is going home to __New York__.
7.

They are leaving from Gate _____.
8.

They are leaving _____ airplane.
9.

Answers: 1. They wait for the bus.   2. They get on the bus.   3. They pay the fare.
4. They ask for a transfer.   5. They change to another bus.
6. They get off the bus at the beach.   7. New York   8. 68   9. by

165

Review 14

The Lee family wants to go to the beach by bus. They wait on the corner for the bus. They get on the bus. They pay the fare and ask for a transfer. The bus goes south on Western Ave. They get off at Pico Blvd. and change to another bus. The bus goes west for about 15 miles. The Lee family gets off the bus at the beach.

1. The Lee family goes to the beach by bus.   (Yes)   No
2. They ask for the fare.   Yes   No
3. The bus goes south on Western Ave.   Yes   No
4. They get off at Western Ave.   Yes   No
5. The bus goes north for about 15 miles.   Yes   No
6. They get off the bus at the beach.   Yes   No

Answers: 1. Yes 2. No 3. Yes 4. No 5. No 6. Yes

Getting Around the City

ARRIVALS				
FLIGHT	FROM	SCHEDULED	ARRIVAL	GATE
163	Phoenix	1:30	1:45	63
210	Denver	11:00	ON TIME	22
104	Honolulu	12:45	ON TIME	25

1. Where does Flight 163 come from?
   It comes from ___Phoenix___.

2. What time does it arrive?
   It arrives at _____.

3. At what gate does it arrive?
   It arrives at Gate_____.

4. Where does Flight 104 come from?
   _____

5. What time does it arrive?
   _____

6. At what gate does it arrive?
   _____

Answers: 1. Phoenix   2. 1:45   3. 63   4. It comes from Honolulu.   5. It arrives at 12:45.
6. It arrives at Gate 25.

Your Notes

Unit 15

Money

Lesson 15a

Objectives: name coins and bills
ask for change

These are the names for U.S. coins.

- a penny  — pennies
- a nickel  — nickels 
- a dime  — dimes 
- a quarter  — quarters 

- a one-dollar bill (a one) — ones
- a five-dollar bill (a five) — fives 
- a ten-dollar bill (a ten) — tens 
- a twenty-dollar bill (a twenty) — twenties 

These are the names for bills.

170

Money

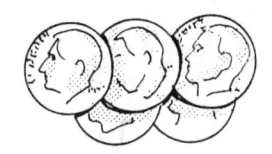

1. quarters
2. _____
3. _____

4. _____
5. _____
6. _____

Sue: Excuse me. Do you have change for a dollar?

Stranger: No, Sorry.

Sue: Thanks, anyway.

Sue: Excuse me. Do you have change for a dollar?

Stranger: Yes. Here you are.

Sue: Thanks.

Sue wants to use the telephone. She needs change.

Answers: 1. quarters 2. dimes 3. nickels 4. a five-dollar bill (a five)
5. a twenty-dollar bill (a twenty) 6. tens

Lesson 15b

Objective — ask about prices

Minh wants to buy a jacket for her husband.

cash — check — charge or credit card

Minh: How much is this?

Saleslady: $37.95.

Minh: Okay. I'll take it.

Saleslady: Cash or charge?

Minh: Cash.

We say prices two different ways.

How much is this? — 3 dollars and 9 cents. — 3-0-9 — $3.09

How much is this?

1. 19 dollars and 99 cents
2. 19 - 99
3. ___ dollars and ___ cents
4.
5. ___ dollars and ___ cents
6.

Answers: 1. 19 dollars and 99 cents 2. 19 - 99 3. 16 dollars and 75 cents 4. 16 - 75 5. 48 dollars and 50 cents 6. 48 - 50

Money

Sue went to the sale rack.

How much is this?

½ PRICE SALE

It's half the price marked. It's on sale for $25.

$50

Everything is on sale for ½ price.

What is the price marked?

How much is it on sale?

1. $40
2. $20

What is the price marked?

How much is it on sale?

3. _____
4. _____

What is the price marked?

How much is it on sale?

5. _____
6. _____

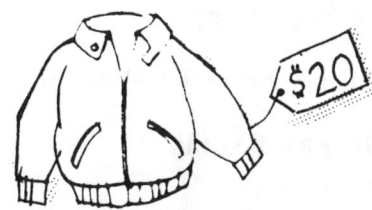

What is the price marked?

How much is it on sale?

7. _____
8. _____

Answers: 1. $40   2. $20   3. $60   4. $30   5. $100   6. $50   7. $20   8. $10

173

Lesson 15c

Objective: learn how to buy a money order

Sue and Minh are at the post office.

You can buy many things at the post office.

stamps   post card   aerogram   money order

Minh wants to buy a money order to pay her gas bill.

Postal Clerk: Next.

Minh: I want to pay my gas bill. I need to buy a money order for $30.00.

Postal Clerk: That's $30.00 plus a dollar fee. That'll be $31.00.

fee = a price you pay to buy a money order

1. Minh is at the market.	Yes	No
2. Minh wants to buy stamps.	Yes	No
3. Minh wants to pay her telephone bill.	Yes	No
4. Minh needs to pay $31.00.	Yes	No

Answers: 1. No 2. No 3. No 4. Yes

Money

The postal clerk tells Minh what to do.

Postal Clerk: Now, fill this in. Keep the top and send the bottom.

Minh: Thanks.

Postal Clerk: Have a nice day.

Minh: You, too.

---

fill in = write

keep =

send =

top

bottom

Look at the gas bill on page 174. Fill in the customer receipt.

Customer Receipt # 3796276
$30.00

Pay To **Gas Co.**   Purchaser **Minh Ly**
Street **P.O. Box 34**   Street **1323**
City ___ State ___ Zip **91783**   City ___ State ___ Zip **91411**
    2.   3.   5.   6.

Answers: 1. Gas Co.   2. Reseda   3. CA   4. S. Elm Ave. # 2E   5. Van Nuys   6. CA

175

Lesson 15d

Objective ask to borrow money

Sue and Minh are at a restaurant.

Sue's lunch is $5.50. She only has $4.50 in her purse. She has to borrow money.

Sue: Oh, no! I only have $4.50. Can I borrow a dollar?

Minh: Sure, here.

Sue: Thanks. I'll pay you back tomorrow.

1. Sue and Minh are at a restaurant.   Yes   No
2. Sue needs to borrow $2.00.   Yes   No
3. Minh gives Sue money.   Yes   No
4. Sue will pay back Minh tomorrow.   Yes   No

Answers: 1. Yes   2. No   3. Yes   4. Yes

176

Money

Sue: Oh, __no__! I _____ have $4.50. Can I
          1.   2.
_____ a _____ ?
      3.   4.

Minh: Sure, _____ .
           5.

Sue: Thanks. I'll _____ you back _____ .
                  6.   7.

"Lunch is $5.50. How much do I need to borrow?"

I only have $4.50.
I need to borrow
__$1.00__
  8.

I only have $2.50.
I need to borrow
_____
  9.

I only have $3.00.
I need to borrow
_____
  10.

I only have $4.00.
I need to borrow
_____
  11.

I only have $3.50.
I need to borrow
_____
  12.

Answers: 1. no 2. only 3. borrow 4. dollar 5. here 6. pay 7. tomorrow 8. $1.00 9. $3.00 10. $2.50 11. $1.50 12. $2.00.

177

Review 15

Sue and Minh did many things downtown. They went to a clothing store, the post office and a restaurant. Sue bought a jacket on sale for her husband.

At the post office, Minh bought a money order to pay her gas bill. She didn't buy stamps or postcards. Sue needed to borrow money at the restaurant. She will pay back Minh tomorrow.

1. Sue and Minh went downtown.	(Yes)	No
2. They went to church.	Yes	No
3. Sue bought a shirt for her husband.	Yes	No
4. At the post office Minh bought a money order.	Yes	No
5. Minh borrowed money from Sue.	Yes	No
6. Tomorrow Sue will go to the market.	Yes	No

Answers: 1. Yes 2. No 3. No 4. Yes 5. No 6. No

Money

1. a penny 
2. _____ 
3. _____

4. _____
5. _____ 
6. _____ 

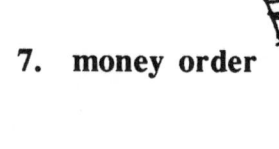

7. money order — c
8. cash
9. stamps
10. aerogram
11. check
12. credit card

a. 
b. 
c. 
d. 
e. 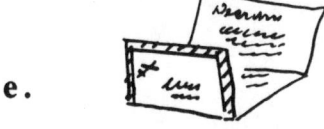
f.

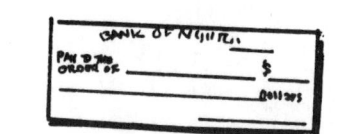

Answers: 1. a penny 2. a nickel 3. a dime 4. a quarter 5. a five-dollar bill 6. a ten-dollar bill
7. c 8. d 9. a 10. e 11. f 12. b

179

Your Notes

Unit 16

The Telephone

Lesson 16a

Objectives: ask for the telephone / use the telephone

"We can ask to use the telephone in different ways."

"May I use the telephone?" — "Sure, go ahead."

"Can I make a telephone call?" — "Of course you can. It's in the kitchen."

"These are the parts of a telephone."

- cord
- receiver
- dial

1. _____ 2. _____ 3. _____

Answers: 1. dial 2. cord 3. receiver

182

The Telephone

Pick it up.

Answer it.

Hang it up.

When the telephone rings, this is what we do.

1.   2.   3.

You can ask "Information" for a telephone number.

What city, please?

Los Angeles. I'd like the number for Tom Wilson.

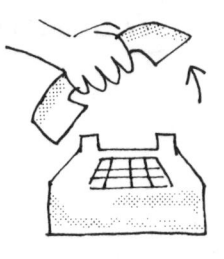

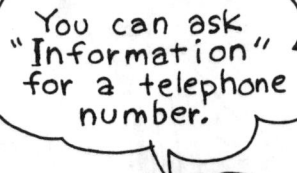

Operator: What city, please?
Mr. Snachez: Los Angeles. I'd like the number for Tom Wilson.
Operator: Spell the last name, please.
Mr. Sanchez: W - I - L - S - O - N.
Operator: Thank you for calling. The number is 555-3876.

Answers: 1. Hang it up.   2. Pick it up.   3. Answer it.

Lesson 16b

Objectives: order food
leave messages
recognize wrong numbers

This is what we do at a public telephone.

Pick up receiver.
Listen for dial tone.
Deposit coins.
Hang it up.

Hi. Is this the Pizza Place?

The Sanchez family wants to order take-out pizza.

Mr. Sanchez: Hi. Is this the Pizza Place?

Restaurant: Yes, it is.

Mr. Sanchez: I'd like to order a large pizza with sausage.

Restaurant: Your address, please?

Mr. Sanchez: It's 631 Forrest Blvd.
Could you send extra napkins, please?

Restaurant: Sure. That'll be 30 minutes.

The Telephone

1. I'd like to order Chinese food.
   Could you send extra fortune cookies?

2. I'd like to order chicken.
   Could you send extra napkins?

3. I'd like to order potatoes.
   Could you send extra napkins?

a.

b.

c.

Marty Sanchez: Hi. This is Marty Sanchez.
I'd like to speak to Miss Lee.

Other Person: I'm sorry. You have the wrong number.

Marty Sanchez: Is this 555-0742?

Other Person: No, it isn't.

Marty Sanchez: I'm sorry.

Marty Sanchez: Hi. This _____ Marty Sanchez.
4.
I'd _____ to _____ to Miss Lee.
5.   6.

Other Person: I'm _____. You _____ the
7.   8.
_____ number.
9.

Marty Sanchez: Is _____ 555-0742?
10.

Other Person: No, _____ isn't.
11.

Marty Sanchez: I'm sorry.

Answers: 1. b 2. c 3. a 4. is 5. like 6. speak 7. sorry 8. have 9. wrong 10. this 11. it

185

Lesson 16c

Objective — take a telephone message

Speech bubbles:
- Miss Powers wants to talk with her doctor.
- The doctor is not in. Sara has to take a message.
- May I speak to Dr. Stein?
- I'm sorry. He isn't in.

Message pad:
To Dr. Stein
Date 5/12 Time 2:35
WHILE YOU WERE OUT
Miss Powers
Telephone No. 555-1649
✓ TELEPHONED   PLEASE CALL BACK ✓
Received Call: Sara

Miss Powers: May I speak to Dr. Stein?

Sara: I'm sorry. He isn't in. May I take a message?

Miss Powers: Yes. This is Karen Powers. Please ask the doctor to call me. My number is 555-1649.

Sara: All right, Miss Powers. That's 555-1649.

Miss Powers: Thank you. Good-bye.

---

1. Who wants to speak to Dr. Stein? ✎ Karen Powers
2. Is the doctor in? _____
3. Who takes the message? _____
4. What is Karen Powers' telephone number? _____

186   Answers: 1. Karen Powers   2. No, he isn't.   3. Sara   4. 555-1649

The Telephone

Susie wants to talk to her friend Marty. Mrs. Sanchez takes a message.

Marty—
Susie called.
Call her at
555-0837
—mom—

Susie: Hi. Is Marty there?

Mrs. Sanchez: I'm sorry. He isn't here now. May I take a message?

Susie: Yes. Tell Marty to call me. This is Susie. My number is 555-0837.

1. Who is calling Marty? __Susie__
2. Is Marty at home?_____
3. Who takes the message?_____
4. What is Susie's telephone number?_____

Answers: 1. Susie   2. No, he isn't.   3. Mrs. Sanchez   4. 555-0837

Lesson 16d

Objectives: ask for information / talk about the future

Calvin is calling John, but he's not home. Calvin says he will call back later.

Is John there?

No, he isn't.

Calvin: Is John there?
Other Person: No, he isn't.
Calvin: Okay. I'll call back later.

Calvin: Is John **there** ?
                    1.
Other Person: No, he _____ .
                             2.
Calvin: Okay. _____ call
                     3.
back _____ .
          4.

I'll	=	I will
He'll	=	He will
She'll	=	She will

188   Answers: 1. there 2. isn't 3. I'll 4. later

The Telephone

Richard: Hi. This is Richard. Is Sandra in?
Other Person: No, she isn't. She'll be home at 2 o'clock.

1. Who is Richard calling? _Sandra_
2. What time will she be home?
   _____

Mrs. Price: This is Mrs. Price. May I talk to Mr. Turner?
Other Person: I'm sorry. He's not in.
Mrs. Price: What time will he be in?
Other Person: He'll be in around 11:00.

3. Who is Mrs. Price calling? _____
4. What time will he be in?
   _____

Dorothy: Good morning. This is Dorothy. Is Janie there?
Other Person: No, I'm sorry. She'll be back in an hour. Will you call back later?
Dorothy: Yes, I will.

5. Who is Dorothy calling? _____
6. What time will she be back?
   _____

Answers: 1. Sandra 2. She'll be home at 2 o'clock. 3. Mr. Turner 4. He'll be in around 11:00.
5. Janie 6. She'll be back in an hour.

Review 16

Dorothy has to make some telephone calls today. In the morning, she'll call her doctor to make an appointment. She wants to see her next week.

In the afternoon, she'll call her friend Susie to ask her to come for dinner. If Susie is not home, she'll leave a message with Susie's mother to call her back.

In the evening, she'll call Crispy Fried Chicken to order take-out chicken. She'll ask for extra napkins. Dorothy does not like to dial wrong numbers so she'll dial slowly.

1. Dorothy will call her doctor today.	(Yes)	No
2. She wants to see her next month.	Yes	No
3. Dorothy will also call her friend.	Yes	No
4. Dorothy will call back later if her friend is not at home.	Yes	No
5. Dorothy will order pizza on the telephone.	Yes	No
6. She'll ask for extra napkins.	Yes	No
7. Dorothy dials wrong numbers a lot because she dials too fast.	Yes	No

Answers: 1. Yes 2. No 3. Yes 4. No 5. No 6. Yes 7. No

The Telephone

John: Hello. This is John Miko. Is Dr. Johnson there?

Receptionist: No, he's not in the office. May I take a message?

John: Please tell him to call me back. My telephone number is 555-0767.

```
To  Dr. Johnson           1.
Date_____ Time_____
WHILE YOU WERE OUT
Miss
Mr.
Mrs.            2.
of _____
Telephone No. (___)_____ Ext._____
                3.
```

```
To _____  4.
Date_____ Time_____
WHILE YOU WERE OUT
Miss
Mr.
Mrs.            5.
of _____
Telephone No. (___)_____ Ext._____
                6.
```

Rita: Hello. This is Rita Lee. Is Mr. Manning in?

Receptionist: I'm sorry. He isn't. May I take a message?

Rita: Can he call me back? I'm at (818) 555-7666.

Mary: Hello. I want to talk to Mrs. Ramirez. This is Mary Takehara.

Secretary: I'm sorry, Mary. Mrs. Ramirez is not in. Do you want her to call you back?

Mary: Yes, please. My number is (213) 555-3882.

```
To _____  7.
Date_____ Time_____
WHILE YOU WERE OUT
Miss
Mr.
Mrs.            8.
of _____
Telephone No. (___)_____ Ext._____
                9.
```

Answers: 1. Dr. Johnson 2. John Miko 3. 555-0767 4. Mr. Manning 5. Rita Lee 6. (818) 555-7666
7. Mrs. Ramirez 8. Mary Takehara 9. (213) 555-3882

Your Notes

Unit 17

Emergencies

Lesson 17a

Objectives — identify an emergency; report an emergency

Fred was looking out his window. He saw a burglar going into Ramiro's house. He called 9-1-1.

In an emergency, call 9-1-1.

emergency = when the situation is dangerous or you need help immediately

1. If you see a fire, call 911.

2. If you need the highway patrol, police or sheriff, call 911.

3. If you need help when someone is very ill or hurt badly, call 911.

a. (highway patrol car)

b. (fire truck)

c. (ambulance)

194

Answers: 1. b 2. a 3. c

Emergencies

Call 9-1-1 to report these emergencies:

a fire

a woman with a gun

a man hurt badly

a man having a heart attack

a child swallowed pills

What are you reporting?

A man is hurt badly. He's bleeding.

When you call 911 from a public telephone:
- You don't need any money.
- You must give the address.
- The address is written on the telephone.
- Say the numbers of the address very slowly and clearly.

1. _____
2. _____
3. _____

Answers: 1. a woman with a gun 2. a fire 3. a man having a heart attack

Lesson 17b

Objective — learn how to talk to the police

In some emergencies, the police come. They will fill out a report. They will ask many questions.

1. Do you have any identification?

    a.

2. What is your age? When were you born?

    b.

3. What is your telephone number?

    c.

4. What is your work address?

    d.

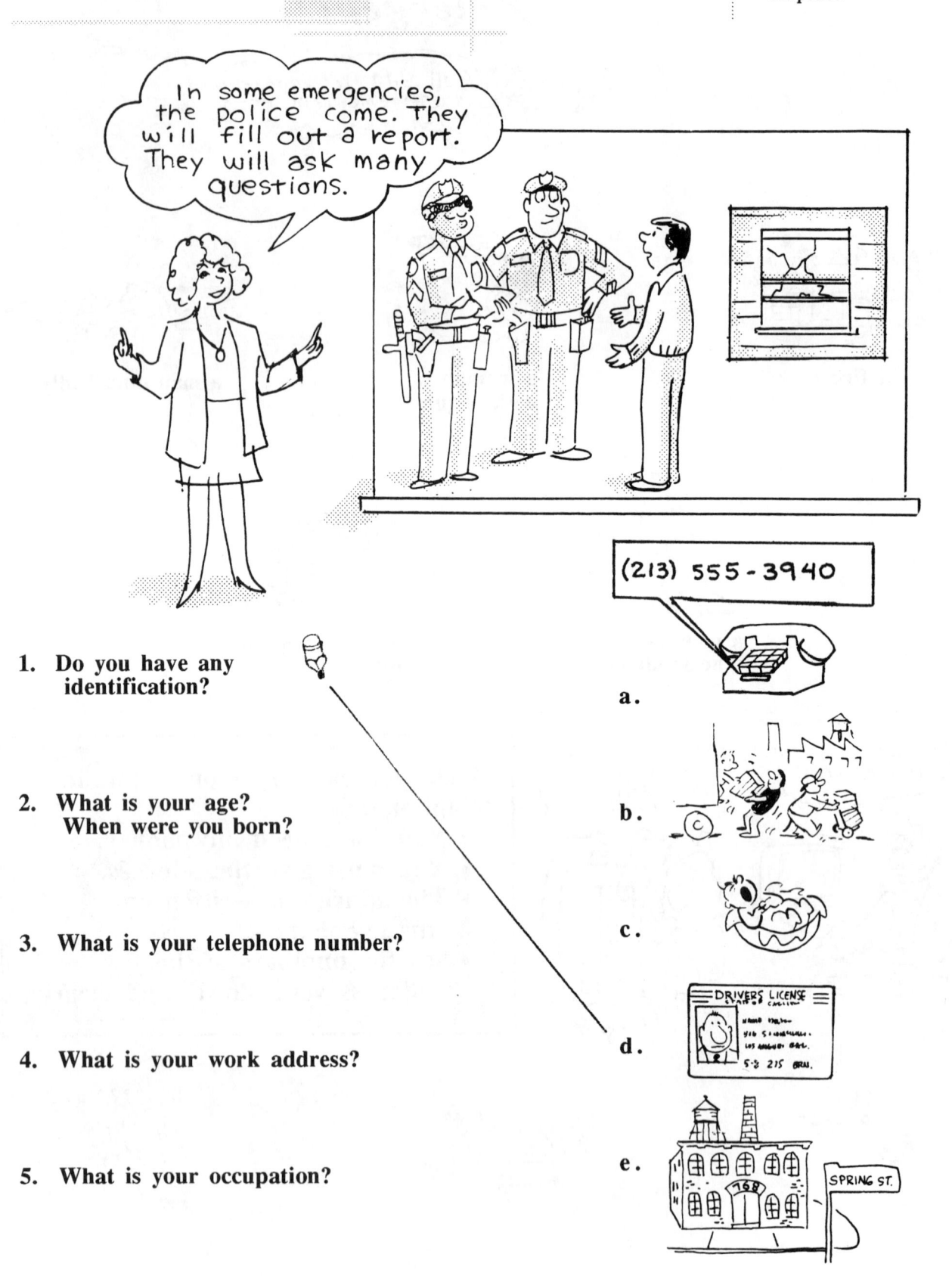

5. What is your occupation?

    e.

Answers: 1. d 2. c 3. a 4. e 5. b

196

Emergencies

Did anyone see what happened?

1. Did anyone see what happened?

2. When did it happen?

3. How did the burglar get in?

4. What was taken?

5. Do you have the brand, serial number, or model number?

6. Write down any other items that are missing.

_____ _____ _____
      1.   2.   3.

I'm sorry. I don't understand. Could you repeat that, please?

I'm sorry. I don't understand. Could you speak a little slower, please?

If you don't understand the police officer, this is what you say.

Answers: 1. Did anyone see what happened? 2. What was taken? 3. Write down any other items that are missing.

197

Lesson 17c

Objective: learn what to do if the police stop you

Fred was driving his car too fast.

Fred heard the siren and he saw the flashing lights of a police car. This is what he had to do:

1. Pull over to the side of the road and stop as soon as it is safe.

2. Turn off his car.

3. Keep his hands on the steering wheel.

4. Follow directions.

Emergencies

Police Officer: Good afternoon. May I see your driver's license?
Fred: Good afternoon. Here it is.
Police Officer: Do you know why I stopped you?
Fred: Yes. I was driving too fast.
Police Officer: I have to give you a ticket. Please be more careful next time.
Fred: Okay. I will.
Police Officer: The ticket tells you when and where to appear in court.

Police Officer: Good afternoon. May I see your __driver's license__?
1.
Fred: Good afternoon. Here it is.
Police Officer: Do you know why I _____ you?
2.
Fred: Yes. I was driving too _____ .
3.
Police Officer: I have to give you a _____ .
4.
Please be more careful next time.
Fred: Okay. I will.
Police Officer: The ticket tells you _____ and _____
5.   6.
to appear in _____ .
7.

Answers: 1. driver's license 2. stopped 3. fast 4. ticket 5. when 6. where 7. court

199

Lesson 17d

Objective: read safety signs

Fred is at work. He sees safety signs.

DO NOT INHALE FUMES	= Don't breathe it.
KEEP OUT	= Don't go in here.
OUT OF ORDER	= It doesn't work.
EMPLOYEES ONLY	= Don't go in here if you don't work here.

1. KEEP OUT — a. It doesn't work.
2. EMPLOYEES ONLY — b. Don't go in here.
3. DO NOT INHALE FUMES — c. Don't breathe it.
4. OUT OF ORDER — d. Don't go in here if you don't work here.

Answers: 1. b 2. d 3. c 4. a

200

Emergencies

NO SMOKING	= Don't smoke here.
DO NOT USE NEAR HEAT	= Don't use it where it's hot.
HANDLE WITH CARE	= Be careful when you use it.
POISON	= Don't drink or eat it.

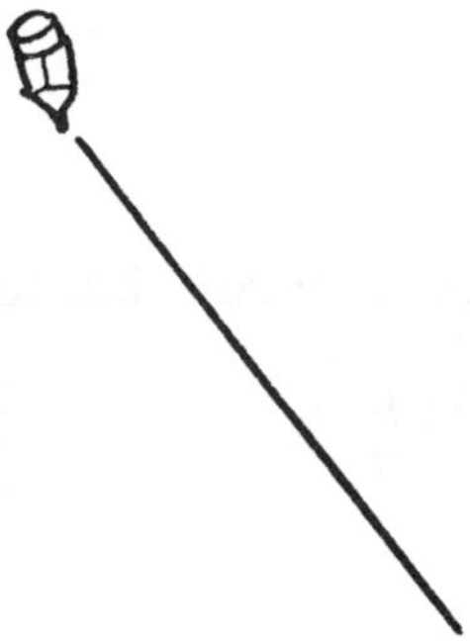

1. HANDLE WITH CARE
2. NO SMOKING
3. DO NOT USE NEAR HEAT
4. POISON

a. Don't smoke here.

b. Don't use it where it's hot.

c. Be careful when you use it.

d. Don't drink or eat it.

Answers: 1. c 2. a 3. b 4. d

Review 17

Fred had a terrible day! He was looking out his window and he saw a burglar break a window and go into Ramiro's house. Fred knew Ramiro wasn't home. This was an emergency, so he called 911. After Ramiro returned home, two police officers came to talk to him. They asked Ramiro many questions about what happened and what the burglar took.

Later that day, Fred was driving his car. He was thinking about the burglar. He was still nervous, and he was not thinking about his driving. Suddenly, he heard a siren, and he saw the flashing lights of a police car. He pulled over to the side of the road and stopped as soon as it was safe. He turned off his car. He was very nervous, but he kept his hands on the steering wheel. He waited for the police officer's instructions. The police officer told Fred he was driving too fast. He gave Fred a ticket and told him to appear in court. Fred was very friendly and polite to the police officer. What a day for Fred!

1. Fred saw a burglar go into Ramiro's house.   (Yes)   No
2. A burglar broke Fred's window.   Yes   No
3. Ramiro was at home.   Yes   No
4. Ramiro called 911.   Yes   No
5. The police officer stopped Fred because he was driving too fast.   Yes   No
6. Fred was driving very carefully.   Yes   No
7. The police officer gave Fred a ticket.   Yes   No

Answers: 1. Yes 2. No 3. No 4. No 5. Yes 6. No 7. Yes

Emergencies

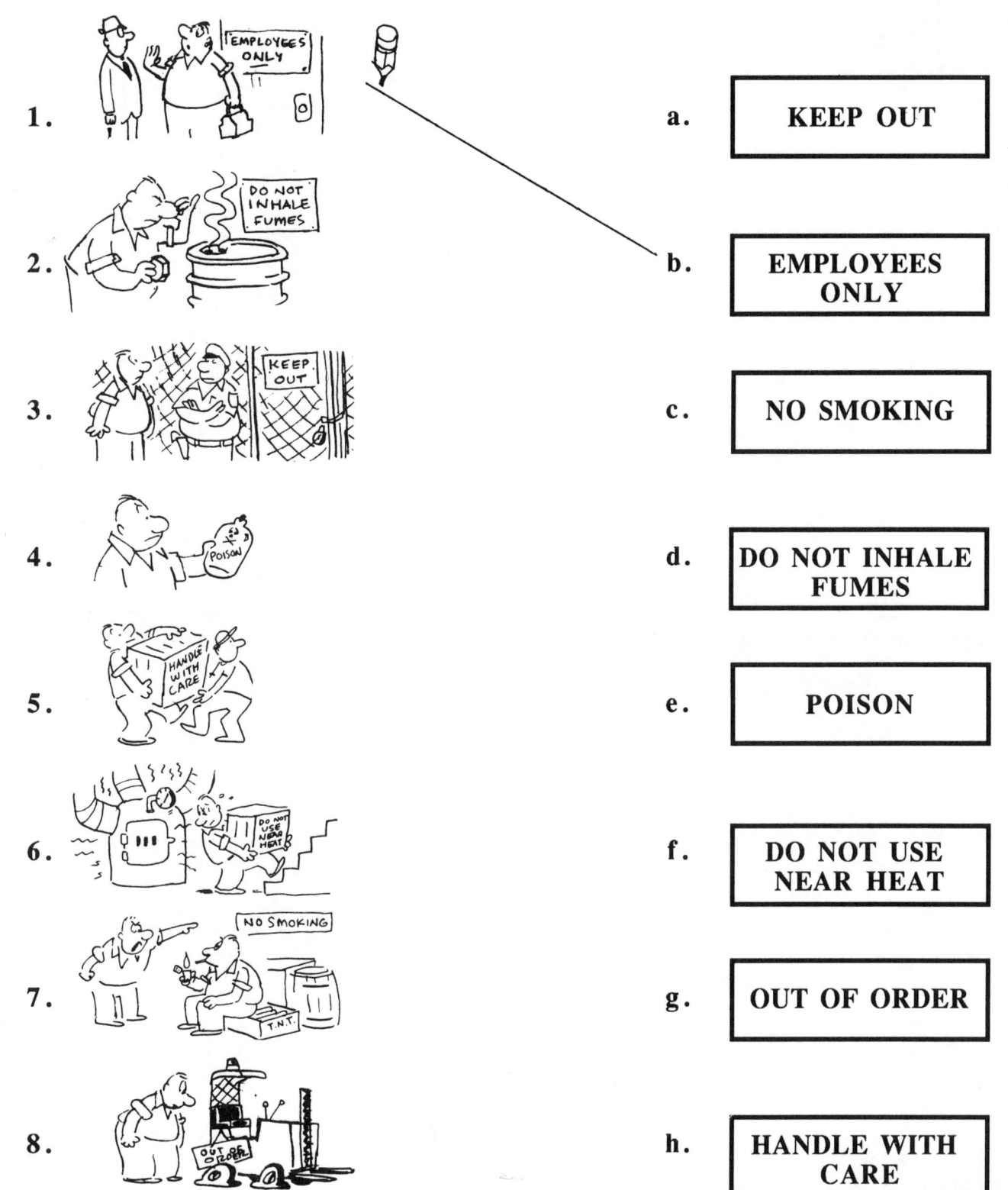

1. a. KEEP OUT

2. b. EMPLOYEES ONLY

3. c. NO SMOKING

4. d. DO NOT INHALE FUMES

5. e. POISON

6. f. DO NOT USE NEAR HEAT

7. g. OUT OF ORDER

8. h. HANDLE WITH CARE

Answers: 1. b 2. d 3. a 4. e 5. h 6. f 7. c 8. g

203

Your Notes

Unit 18

Schools

Lesson 18a

Objective | learn about different kinds of schools

Tim Lee is asking Joe Sanchez about schools in the neighborhood.

Tim Lee: I need to find schools for my children. Can you help?

Joe Sanchez: Of course. How old are they?

Tim Lee: June is 8, Sam is 13, and Tom is 16.

Joe Sanchez: June has to go to an elementary school. Elm Street School is just two blocks away.

1. How old is June?   June is 8.

2. How old is Tom?   _____

3. How old is Sam?   _____

4. What is the name of the elementary school?   _____

5. Where is the elementary school?   _____

206   Answers: 1. June is 8.   2. Tom is 16.   3. Sam is 13.   4. Elm Street School.   5. Two blocks away.

Schools

Schools have different grades for different ages.

Grades 1-6	Grades 7-9	Grades 10-12	
Ages 6-11	Ages 12-14	Ages 15-18	18+ years old
Elementary school	Jr. high school	Sr. high school	Adult school

13 years old — Sam has to go to __junior high__ school.
1.

8 years old — June has to go to _____ school.
2.

16 years old — Tom has to go to _____ school.
3.

45 years old — Tim Lee should go to _____ school.
4.

Jr. = Junior
Sr. = Senior

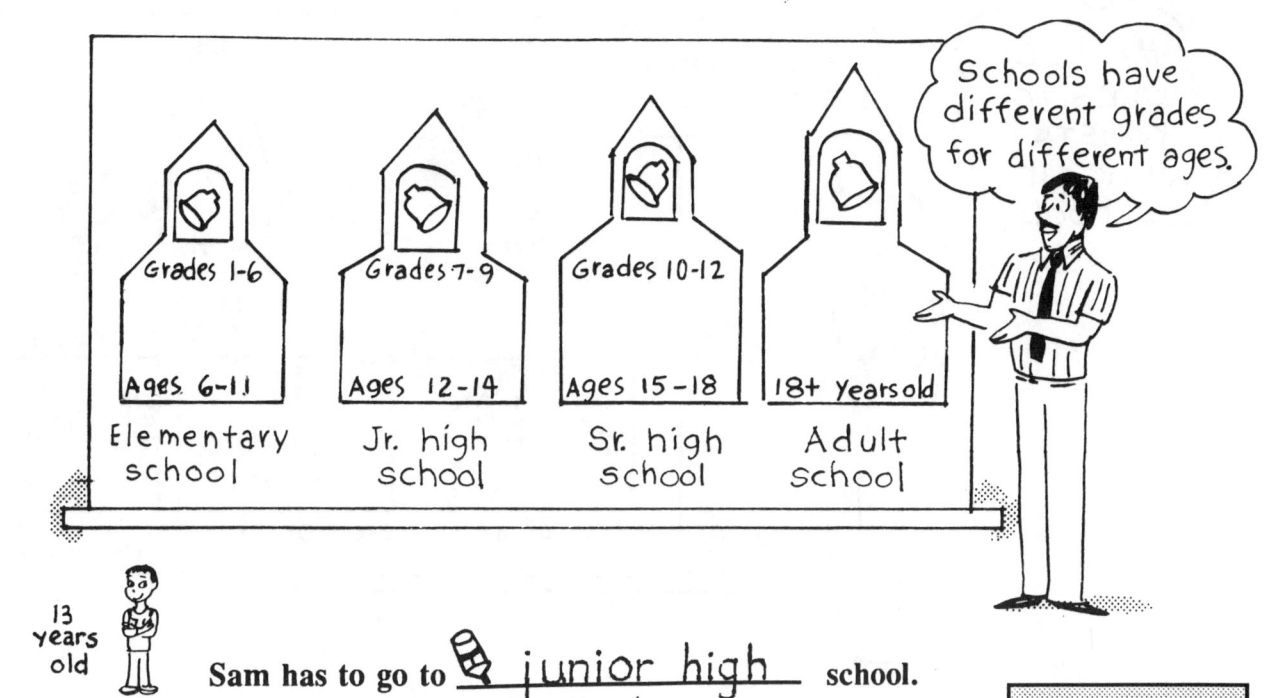

has to = It is necessary.
should = It is good for you.

A child *has to* go to school.
An adult *should*

Answers: 1. junior high 2. elementary 3. senior high 4. adult

207

Lesson 18b

Objective: learn how to register at schools

Mrs. Lee wants to register June in school.

These are the papers she needs.

- Birth Certificate — proof of age
- Gas-electric Bill — proof of address
- proof of immunization

Clerk: Is this a new student?

Mrs. Lee: Yes. We're from Taiwan.

Clerk: Did you bring any papers with you?

Mrs. Lee: What do I need?

Clerk: You need proof of age, proof of address, and proof of immunization.

What papers does Mrs. Lee need for her daughter?

1. proof of age
2. _____
3. _____

Is she a new student?

4. _____

Where is she from?

5. _____

208 Answers: 1. proof of age 2. proof of address 3. proof of immunization 4. Yes, she is. 5. Taiwan

Schools

Mr. and Mrs. Lee want to learn English in adult school.

Mr. Lee: We want an English class.

Clerk: Did you study English in your country?

Mr. Lee: A little. We want to practice conversation.

Clerk: Okay. Fill out this registration form.

Here is the information you need.

Fill out this registration form for Mr. Lee.

Name: Tim Lee
Address: 146 Rose St.
City: Los Angeles
State: California
Zip: 90046
Telephone: (213) 555-3316
Date of Birth: May 5, 1946

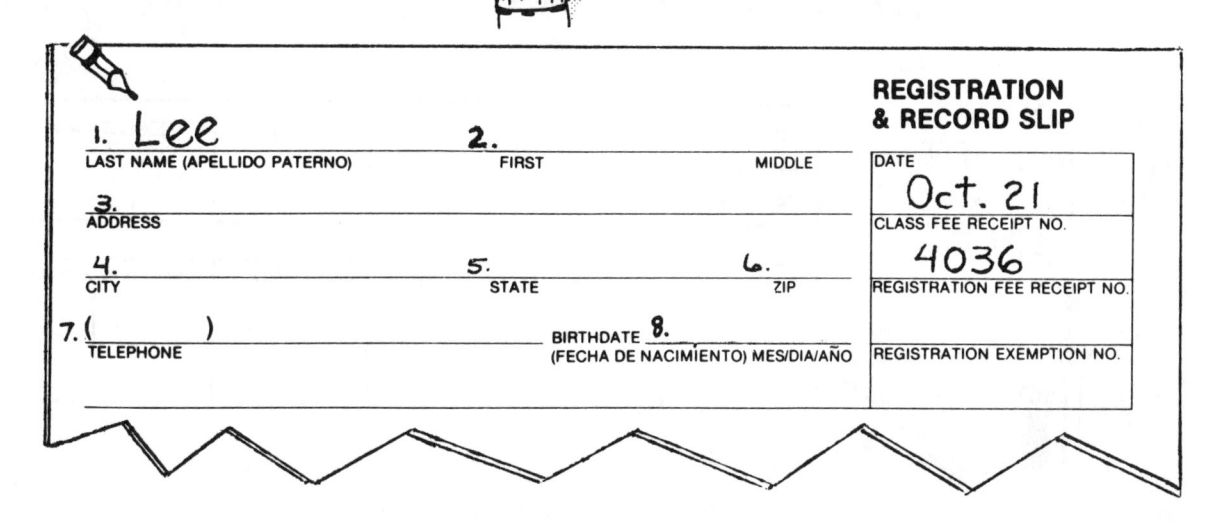

REGISTRATION & RECORD SLIP

1. Lee
LAST NAME (APELLIDO PATERNO)
2. _____ FIRST
_____ MIDDLE

DATE
Oct. 21

3. _____
ADDRESS

CLASS FEE RECEIPT NO.
4036

4. _____ CITY
5. _____ STATE
6. _____ ZIP

REGISTRATION FEE RECEIPT NO.

7. ( ) _____
TELEPHONE
BIRTHDATE 8. _____
(FECHA DE NACIMIENTO) MES/DIA/AÑO

REGISTRATION EXEMPTION NO.

Answers: 1. Lee 2. Tim 3. 146 Rose St. 4. Los Angeles 5. California 6. 90046
7. (213) 555-3316 8. May 5, 1946

Lesson 18c

Objectives: learn about the people who work in a school; find places on a map

Tom is talking to his teacher.

Tom: I'd like to go to college in the East.

Teacher: You should talk to the counselor.

Tom: Where's the counselor's office?

Teacher: It's between Rooms 105 and 107.

1. Does Tom want to go to college? **Yes** No
2. Should he talk to the counselor? Yes No
3. Is the counselor's office next to the principal's office? Yes No

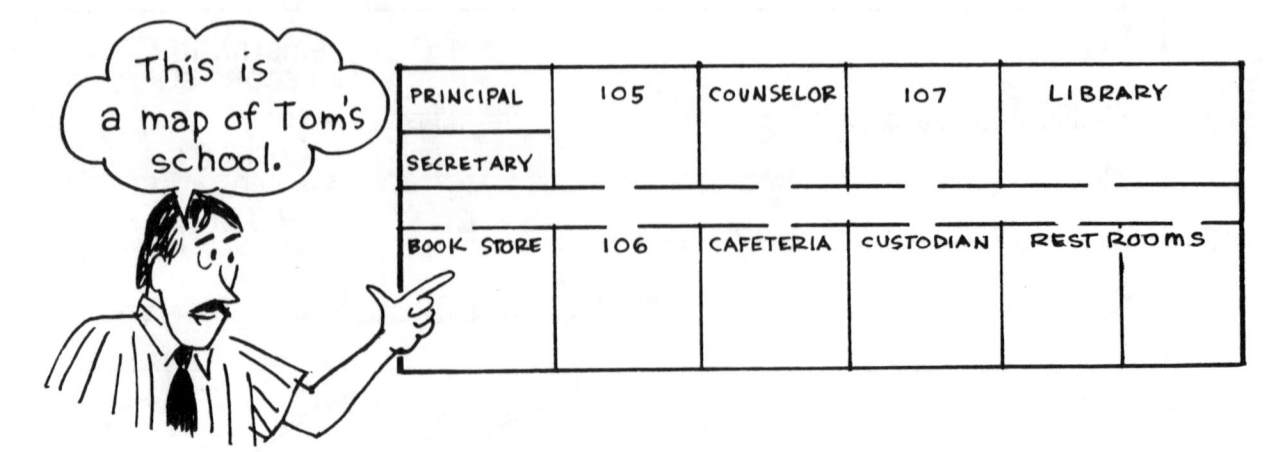

This is a map of Tom's school.

PRINCIPAL	105	COUNSELOR	107	LIBRARY
SECRETARY				
BOOK STORE	106	CAFETERIA	CUSTODIAN	REST ROOMS

Answers: 1. Yes 2. Yes 3. No

Schools

The <u>counselor</u> advises students. The <u>principal</u> directs the school. The <u>secretary</u> manages the office. The <u>custodian</u> cleans the school.

Who is he? **The principal.**
1.
What does he do? _____
2.

Who is she? _____
3.
What does she do? _____
4.

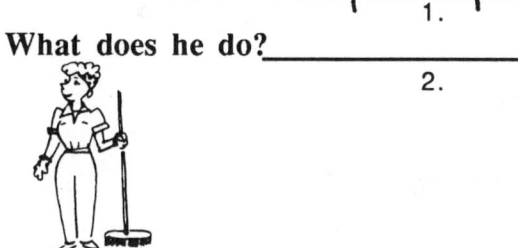

Who is she? _____
5.
What does she do? _____
6.

Who is he? _____
7.
What does he do? _____
8.

Where are these places? Use the map.

9. 
10.  
11.  
12.

a. *Next to the custodian's office.*

b. *Between the custodian's office and Room 106.*

c. *Next to Room 107.*

d. *Across from Room 107.*

Answers: 1. The principal. 2. He directs the school. 3. The secretary. 4. She manages the office. 5. The custodian. 6. She cleans the school. 7. The counselor. 8. He advises the students. 9. c 10. b 11. a 12. d

Lesson 18d

Objectives talk about what you should do in school
talk about what you should not do in school

Sam is in school. His teacher is angry.

Teacher: Sam, are you chewing gum in class?

Sam: Yes. I'm sorry.

Teacher: You should know the rules.
Don't chew gum in class.

What are they doing?

He's chewing gum in school.

She's eating in class.

They're smoking in school.

He's interrupting the class.

He's throwing trash on the floor.

He's speaking Spanish in English class.

Schools

What's he doing?

He's chewing gum in school.

He's speaking Spanish in English class.

What's the rule?

Don't chew gum in school.

Speak only English in English class.

What's the rule?

1. Don't chew gum in school.

2. Don't _____

3. _____

4. _____

5. _____

Answers: 1. Don't chew gum in school. 2. Don't eat in class. 3. Speak only English in English class.
4. Don't smoke in school. 5. Don't interrupt the class.

Review 18

Mr. Lee and Mrs. Lee have 3 children. They have to go to school. They need to have proof of age, proof of address and proof of immunization. The children have to go to different schools because they are different ages. Mr. and Mrs. Lee want to learn more English. They can go to the Adult School. They don't need any papers, but they must fill out a registration form in English. All schools have a principal to direct the school.

1. Mr. and Mrs. Lee have 3 children. (Yes) No
2. The children need papers to go to school. Yes No
3. The children can go to the same school. Yes No
4. Mr. and Mrs. Lee can learn English in the Adult School. Yes No
5. Mr. and Mrs. Lee need proof of address to go to Adult School. Yes No
6. The school secretary directs the school. Yes No

Answers: 1. Yes 2. Yes 3. No 4. Yes 5. No 6. No

Schools

What do they do?

1. the principal
2. the school secretary
3. the custodian
4. the counselor

a. manages the office
b. cleans the school
c. directs the school
d. advises the students

What's the rule?

5.
6.
7.
8.
9.

e. Speak only English in English class.
f. Don't smoke in school.
g. Don't eat in class.
h. Don't chew gum in class.
i. Don't interrupt the class.

Answers: 1. c 2. a 3. b 4. d 5. f 6. i 7. e 8. g 9. h

Your Notes

Unit 19

Driving a Car

Lesson 19a

Objectives learn how to get a learner's permit
learn how to start a car

Tom is going to teach David how to drive. David needs a learner's permit before he learns to drive.

You can get a learner's permit at the Department of Motor Vehicles.

Department of Motor Vehicles = DMV

What do I do?

First, call the DMV for an appointment. Then...

...study the **handbook**.
1.

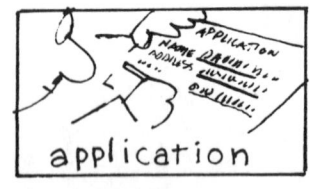

application

Fill out the _____.
2.

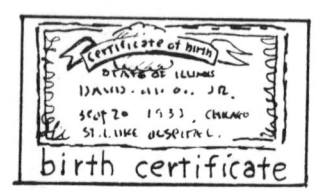

birth certificate

Show your _____.
3.

money

Pay your _____.
4.

written test

Take the _____.
5.

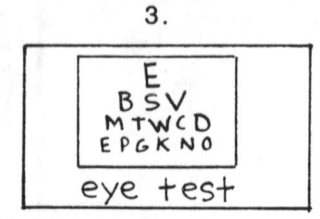

eye test

Take the _____.
6.

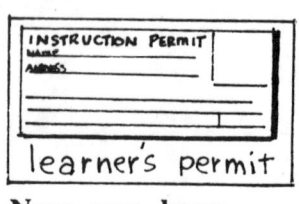

learner's permit

Now you have your _____ _____.
7.

218 Answers: 1. handbook   2. application   3. birth certificate   4. money   5. written test
6. eye test   7. learner's permit

Driving a Car

What do I do now?

David is ready to learn how to drive. Tom and David get in the car.

1. Put on your seat belt.

    ✏️ <u>Put on your seat belt.</u>

2. Adjust the mirrors.

    _____

3. Put the car in park.

    _____

4. Put the key in the ignition.

    _____

5. Start the car. Step on the gas and turn the key.

    _____

Answers: 1. Put on your seat belt. 2. Adjust the mirrors. 3. Put the car in park. 4. Put the key in the ignition.
5. Start the car. Step on the gas and turn the key.

Lesson 19b

Objectives: read road signs
learn how to get a driver's license

David is learning to drive. Tom is giving him directions.

Turn right.

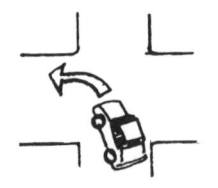

Turn left.    Stop.    Make a U-turn.

What do the signs mean?

You can't turn right.    You can't turn left.    You can't enter. (DO NOT ENTER)   You can go in one direction only. (ONE WAY)

YIELD — You must let the other car go first. 
PED XING — You must stop when people are crossing.
You can't make a U-turn.  
SCHOOL XING — You must stop when people are crossing near a school.

220

Driving a Car

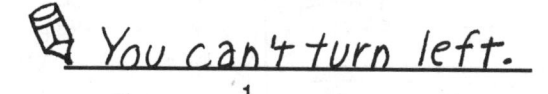

1. ✏️ You can't turn left.

2. _____

3. _____

4. _____

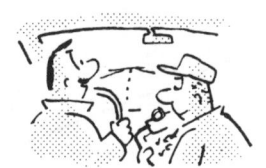

"David is ready to get his driver's license, but he has to do many things first."

Make an appointment.   **Take the driver's test.**   **Get fingerprints taken.**

Get a picture taken.   **Get a driver's license.**

Answers: 1. You can't turn left. 2. You can't make a U-turn. 3. You can't enter. 4. You can't turn right.

221

Lesson 19c

Objective: learn what to do in case of an accident

"Is he a good driver or a bad driver?"

"He's a bad driver. He's not paying attention."

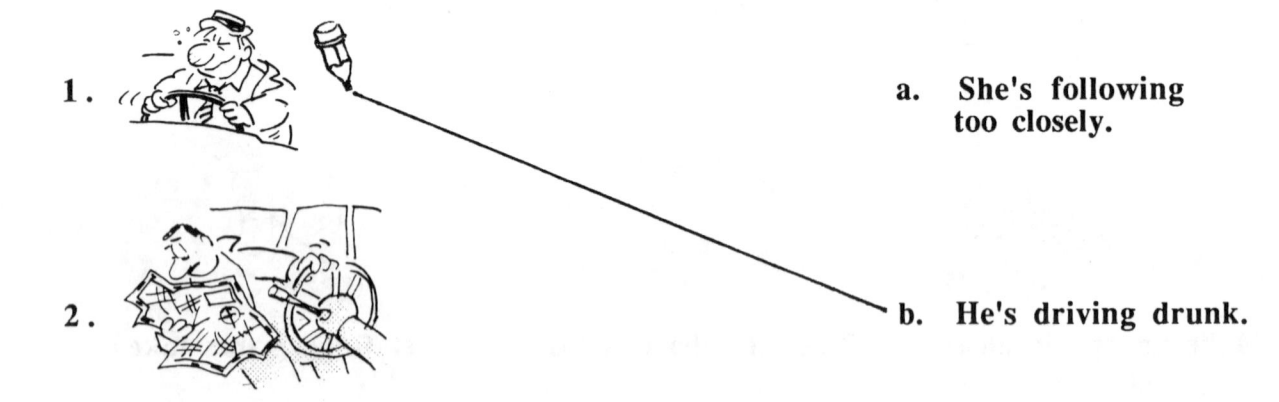

She's a bad driver. She's following too closely.

He's a bad driver. He's driving drunk.

He's a bad driver. He's not paying attention.

1.   a. She's following too closely.

2.   b. He's driving drunk.

3.   c. He's not paying attention.

Answers: 1. b 2. c 3. a

Driving a Car

What happened to David?

He had an accident. They are exchanging information.

David — other driver

David:	Are you hurt?
Other Driver:	No, I'm okay. How about you?
David:	I'm okay, too.
Other Driver:	May I see your driver's license?
David:	Yes, here. May I see yours?
Other Driver:	Sure. Who's your insurance company?
David:	All Nation. Who's yours?
Other Driver:	Century. What's your telephone number?
David:	(818) 555-1312. What's yours?
Other Driver:	(213) 555-6121.

1. Is David hurt? __No.__
2. Does the other driver have a driver's license? _____
3. Who is David's insurance company? _____
4. What is David's telephone number? _____

Answers: 1. No 2. Yes 3. All Nation 4. (818) 555-1312

223

Lesson 19d

Objectives: read parking signs / read a parking ticket

David is looking for a place to park.

Can I park here?

No, the sign says no parking 8am to 5pm school days.

1. It's 4:00 pm on Thursday. Can he park here?   No, he can't.

2. It's 6:00 pm on Thursday. Can he park here?   _____

3. It's 3:00 pm on Saturday. Can he park here?   _____

NO PARKING 9 to 11 am MONDAY

4. It's 10:00 am on Monday. Can he park here?   _____

5. It's 9:00 pm on Tuesday. Can he park here?   _____

6. It's 5:00 pm on Monday. Can he park here?   _____

Answers: 1. No, he can't. 2. Yes, he can. 3. Yes, he can. 4. No, he can't. 5. Yes, he can. 6. Yes, he can.

Driving a Car

David parked here at 4:30 p.m. on Wednesday. He got a ticket.

NO STOPPING
4 to 6 pm
Except Sat. & Sun.

2 HOUR PARKING
8 am to 4 pm
Except Sunday

WARNING
READ POSTED SIGNS
BEFORE PARKING.

Ticket = Parking Violation

1. Did David get a ticket?
   Yes, he did.

2. How much does he have to pay?
   _____

3. Can he send cash?
   _____

4. Can he send a money order?
   _____

5. How many days does David have to pay the ticket?
   _____

Answers: 1. Yes, he did. 2. $28.00 3. No, he can't. 4. Yes, he can. 5. 10 days

Review 19

David wanted to learn how to drive. He asked Tom to teach him. But first, David went to the Department of Motor Vehicles (DMV) and got a learner's permit. Tom taught him how to start the car and then how to drive. David also learned what the road signs mean. Then he went back to the DMV and got his driver's license.

David is happy to have his driver's license, and he wants to be a good driver. He pays attention when he's driving because he doesn't want to have an accident. When he drinks, he doesn't drive. Tom was a good teacher.

1. First, David went to the DMV to get his *learner's   permit* .

2. David learned what the _____ _____ mean.

3. He went back to the _____ and got his driver's license.

4. David doesn't _____ when he drinks.

5. Tom was a good _____.

Answers: 1. learner's permit   2. road signs   3. DMV   4. drive   5. teacher

Driving a Car

1. School Xing
2. a ticket
3. DMV
4. learner's permit
5. Ped Xing
6. school days

a. parking violation
b. instruction permit
c. school crossing
d. Monday-Friday
e. Department of Motor Vehicles
f. pedestrian crossing

Can David turn right?
No, he can't.
7.

Can he turn right?
_____
8.

Can he go if there are no other cars?
_____
9.

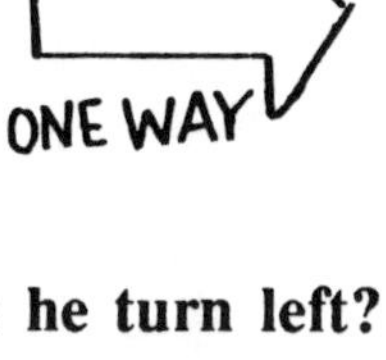

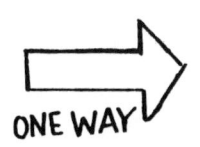

Can he turn left?
_____
10.

Can he make a U turn?
_____
11.

Can he turn left?
_____
12.

Answers: 1. c 2. a 3. e 4. b 5. f 6. d 7. No, he can't. 8. Yes, he can.
9. Yes, he can. 10. No, he can't. 11. No, he can't. 12. No, he can't.

Your Notes

Unit 20

About Government

Lesson 20a

Objective: talk about improving your neighborhood

One of the ways to improve the neighborhood is through the Neighborhood Watch.

The Sanchez family and the Lee family are neighbors. They are going to a meeting of the Neighborhood Watch.

Tim: The streets are very dark at night.
        The street lights are broken.

Joe: We should report it.

Tim: How do we do that?

Joe: We call the Department of Water and Power, the DWP.

About Government

Tim: The streets are dirty.
Joe: *We should report* it.
Tim: How do we do that?
Joe: We can call Public Works.

Tim: The trash cans are full.
Joe: _____ 2.
Tim: _____ 3.
Joe: We can call the Department of Sanitation.

They will = They'll

4. When will they fix the lights?
   They'll fix the lights next week.

   a.

5. When will they sweep the streets?
   They'll sweep the streets next week.

   b.

6. When will they pick up the trash?
   They'll pick up the trash tomorrow.

   c.

Answers: 1. We should report it. 2. We should report it. 3. How do we do that? 4. b 5. c 6. a

Lesson 20b

Objective | talk about resources in the community

Joe is helping Tim learn about the community.

Tim: Is there a park nearby?

Joe: Silver Park is just a mile away.

Tim: What can you do there?

Joe: You can have a picnic and the children can play games or swim.

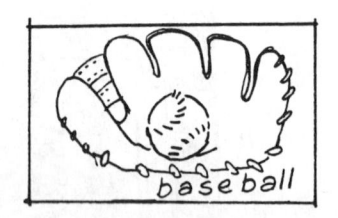

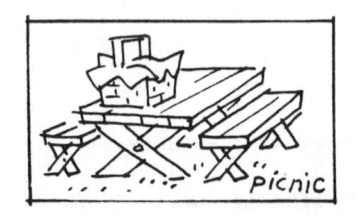

baseball | picnic | tennis

1. You can play baseball.
2. _____
3. _____

play games | handball

The children can

4. _____ . 5. _____

Answers: 1. You can play baseball. 2. You can have a picnic. 3. You can play tennis. 4. play games 5. You can play handball.

About Government

Tim: Is there a _clinic_ nearby?
1.

Joe: Yes, there is a clinic nearby.

Tim: What_____?
2.

Joe: You ____ see a doctor. You can get shots.
3.
Women can get medical care before they have a baby.

Tim: Is there a _____ nearby?
4.

Joe: The Transportation Museum is just a few blocks away.

Tim: _____?
5.

Joe: You _____ see cars, airplanes, boats and many
6.
other things.

Answers: 1. clinic 2. can you do there? 3. can 4. museum
5. What can you do there? 6. can

233

Lesson 20c

Objective: learn about the symbols of the United States of America

This is Uncle Sam. He is a symbol of the United States of America.

symbol = stands for

This is the Statue of Liberty. It stands for freedom and opportunity.

This is the American Eagle. It stands for strength and speed.

1. _____ _____ is a symbol of the USA.

2. The _____ _____ stands for strength and speed.

3. The _____ _____ _____ is a symbol of freedom and opportunity.

Answers: 1. Uncle Sam   2. American Eagle   3. Statue of Liberty

234

About Government

This is the flag of the United States. Sometimes it's called "the stars and stripes."

The "Star Spangled Banner" is our national anthem.

banner = flag
anthem = song

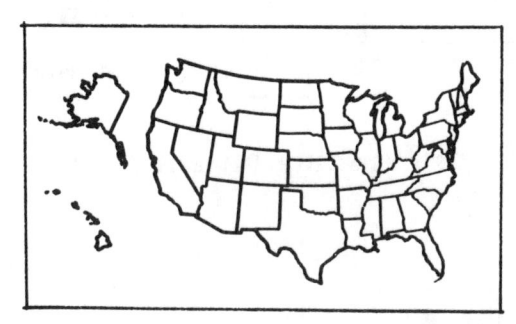

There are 50 stars on the flag.

There are 50 states in the USA.

There is one star for every state.

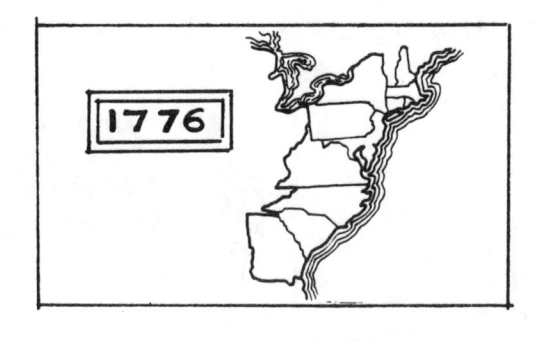

There are 13 stripes on the flag.

In 1776 there were 13 states.

There are 13 stripes for those 13 states.

1. Uncle Sam
2. American Eagle
3. "Star Spangled Banner"
4. flag of the USA
5. Statue of Liberty

a. the national anthem of the USA
b. a symbol of the USA
c. stands for freedom and opportunity
d. stands for strength and speed
e. stars and stripes

Answers: 1. b 2. d 3. a 4. e 5. c

Lesson 20d

Objective: talk about famous places to visit in the USA

Washington, D.C. is the capital of the USA.

The Sanchez family went to Washington, D.C.

White House

Lincoln Memorial

Tim: How was your trip to Washington D.C.

Joe: It was great!

Tim: What did you do there?

Joe: We saw the White House, the Lincoln Memorial, and many other famous places.

They saw the Washington Monument.

What did they do in Washington, D.C.?

Capitol Building

Pentagon

They saw the _Capitol Building_ . _____
    1.   2.

Answers: 1. Capitol Building   2. They saw the Pentagon.

236

About Government

They went to many places in the United States. Where did they go?

They went to the Grand Canyon.

Grand Canyon

San Francisco | New York | Yosemite National Park

1. They went to San Francisco.
2. _____
3. _____

4. The Sanchez family saw the White House in Washington, D.C.	*Yes*	No
5. They saw the Golden Gate Bridge in Washington, D.C.	Yes	No
6. They saw the Pentagon in Washington, D.C.	Yes	No
7. They saw the Lincoln Memorial in New York.	Yes	No
8. They saw many trees in Yosemite National Park.	Yes	No
9. They saw the Washington Monument Washington, D.C.	Yes	No

Answers: 1. They went to San Francisco. 2. They went to New York. 3. They went to Yosemite.
4. Yes 5. No 6. Yes 7. No 8. Yes 9. Yes

237

Review 20

The Lee family and the Sanchez family like their neighborhood. There is a park nearby. The children can play games there. Tim Lee likes to play handball, and Joe Sanchez likes to play tennis at the park.

Sometimes there are problems in the neighborhood. At the Neighborhood Watch meetings, they learn how to improve the neighborhood. If the street lights are broken, they can call the Department of Water and Power. If the streets are dirty, they should call Public Works. If they report the problems in the neighborhood, it will always be a good place to live.

1. The Lee family and the Sanchez family like their _neighborhood_.

2. Tim plays _____ at the _____.

3. They learn how to improve the neighborhood at the _____ _____ meetings.

4. If the street lights are broken, they can call the _____.

5. They should call _____ if the streets are dirty.

Answers: 1. neighborhood 2. handball, park 3. Neighborhood Watch 4. Department of Water and Power 5. Public Works

About Government

1.  a. Grand Canyon
2. b. White House
3. c. Yosemite
4. d. New York
5. e. San Francisco
6. f. Lincoln Memorial

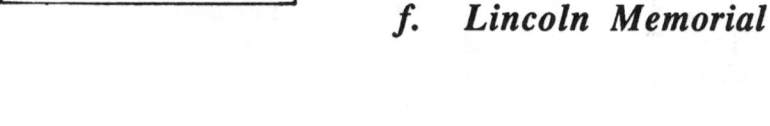

7. Uncle Sam is a symbol of the United States.

8. The Statue of Liberty stands for _____ and _____.

9. The American Eagle is the symbol of _____ and _____.

10. The 50 stars on the flag stand for the 50 _____.

11. The 13 stripes on the flag stand for the first 13 _____.

Answers: 1. b 2. a 3. c 4. d 5. f 6. e 7. United States 8. freedom, opportunity 9. strength, speed 10. states 11. states

239

LEARNING ENGLISH
Lori Howard, Norma Shapiro, and Elaine Sunoo

This series of TV/video lessons and the accompanying *text* use real–life situations to teach ESL. Adults and young adults at the beginning levels can use this independent study program to practice listening, speaking, reading and writing.

Each of the 80 half–hour TV/video lessons corresponds to two work pages in the text. Lessons are grouped into 20 units (4 lessons per unit), each focusing on a different life skill. The *text* provides a review section at the end of each unit.

Learning English makes it simple for students to study independently. The *text* uses easily understood symbols to guide the student through the lesson. In addition, the illustrations in the *text* mirror the visual aids used in the TV/video lesson to help students match what they are reading with what they have learned during the TV/video lesson. To facilitate self–correction, the answers to the exercises appear at the bottom of each page.

Learning English is designed to allow students to learn independently. However, the addition of a teacher or tutor can make the program even more effective. Also the program is well suited for use in a multilevel classroom with one group studying **Learning English** independently while the teacher directs another group.

Units:
- 1—Making Friends
- 2—The Neighborhood
- 3—Health Care
- 4—Looking for Housing
- 5—Marketing
- 6—Recreation and Leisure
- 7—Buying Clothing
- 8—Getting a Job
- 9—On the Job
- 10—Health and Fitness
- 11—Buying a Car
- 12—Apartment Living
- 13—Special Occasions
- 14—Getting Around the City
- 15—Money
- 16—The Telephone
- 17—Emergencies
- 18—Schools
- 19—Driving a Car
- 20—About Government

Text (Units 1–20)	0-937354-76-7
Video Programs	
Video 1 (Unit 1)	0-53-8163
Video 2 (Unit 2)	0-53-8286
Video 3 (Unit 3)	0-53-8342
Video 4 (Unit 4)	0-53-8454
Video 5 (Unit 5)	0-53-8506
Video 6 (Unit 6)	0-53-8675
Video 7 (Unit 7)	0-53-8722
Video 8 (Unit 8)	0-53-8845
Video 9 (Unit 9)	0-53-8965
Video 10 (Unit 10)	0-53-8104
Video 11 (Unit 11)	0-53-8112
Video 12 (Unit 12)	0-53-8125
Video 13 (Unit 13)	0-53-8137
Video 14 (Unit 14)	0-53-8144
Video 15 (Unit 15)	0-53-8156
Video 16 (Unit 16)	0-53-8168
Video 17 (Unit 17)	0-53-8173
Video 18 (Unit 18)	0-53-8187
Video 19 (Unit 19)	0-53-8193
Video 20 (Unit 20)	0-53-8202
Complete Set of 20 Videos	0-53-2027